JOHN 13-21
FROM START2FINISH

MICHAEL WHITWORTH

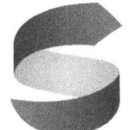

© 2025 by Start2Finish

All rights reserved. No part of this publication may be reproduced, stored in a retrieval system, or transmitted in any form or by any means without the prior written permission of the author. The only exception is brief quotations in printed reviews.

ISBN 978-1-944704-98-8

Published by Start2Finish
Bend, Oregon 97702
start2finish.org

Printed in the United States of America

Unless otherwise noted, all Scripture quotations are from The Holy Bible, English Standard Version®, copyright © 2001 by Crossway Bibles, a publishing ministry of Good News Publishers. Used by permission. All rights reserved.

Cover Design: Evangela Creative

CONTENTS

1.	When Glory Kneels	5
2.	The Way Home	13
3.	Abide in Me	21
4.	Help in the Heat of Hostility	29
5.	The Morning After Sorrow	37
6.	The Prayer of Glory	45
7.	Betrayal & Arrest	55
8.	Behold the Man	63
9.	The Crucifixion of the King	71
10.	Resurrection	79
11.	Peace Be with You	87
12.	Do You Love Me?	95

1

WHEN GLORY KNEELS

JOHN 13

Objective: To show that true glory is revealed through Jesus' humble love and our imitation of it.

INTRODUCTION

Years ago, a missionary in Africa described a local custom: when a guest arrived, the host washed the dust from the traveler's feet. The task wasn't glamorous—it was practical. Long journeys left feet caked with grime, and the washing said, "You're welcome here. You belong." When that missionary told the story to his church back home, one man said, "If that were our custom, I'd never let anyone touch my feet." He spoke for most of us. We like serving, but being served—especially in our weakness—feels unbearable.

John 13 begins with a similar unease. The Son of God rose from supper, removed his robe, and knelt before men who call him Lord. The water in the basin reflected more than dirty feet—it mirrored the humility of heaven. Before Jesus ascended to glory, he stooped to serve. Before he commanded love, he demonstrated it.

This chapter is the hinge of John's Gospel. The ministry of signs gave way to the ministry of sacrifice. The basin replaced the temple; the towel replaced the throne. In this quiet upper room, love took action. Glory would soon shine from a cross, but first, it glimmered from the floor.

When glory knelt, the world finally saw what God had been like all along.

EXAMINATION

Love to the end (13:1–3)

John opens the second half of his Gospel with a line that sets the tone for everything that follows: "Having loved his own who were in the world, he loved them to the end." These words do not merely mark the beginning of the Passion narrative; they define it. The hour had come—the very hour Jesus spoke of throughout chapters 2-12. His signs were complete; now he would be lifted up. What remained was not proof but love—love displayed in its fullest measure.

The phrase "to the end" carries both temporal and qualitative weight. It means Jesus loved them to the last breath and to the uttermost degree. Every word and every movement of the coming hours would demonstrate that divine love is not an emotion but an action. John notes that "the devil had already put it into the heart of Judas Iscariot" (v. 2). Treachery was at the table, yet love remained undiminished. Jesus knew the Father had placed all things in his hands, that he had come from God and was returning to God (v. 3). With that assurance of origin and destiny, he bent low. Divine security freed him for divine humility.

In a world where honor and status governed every interaction, what follows should never have happened. Yet John frames it as the natural outflow of glory. The foot-washing did not diminish Jesus' majesty; it revealed it.

The servant's example (13:4–11)

Without a word of introduction, Jesus rose from the meal, laid aside his outer garments, took a towel, and tied it around his waist. Each verb matters. To lay aside and later take up the garments anticipated his laying down and taking up of life itself (10:17-18). The basin and towel became symbols of the cross—humility that cleanses, service that saves.

Foot-washing was the lowest of household tasks. In Jewish and Greco-Roman culture, even Jewish slaves could be exempted from it; it was that demeaning. No rabbi would stoop so low. Yet Jesus did, shocking the disciples into embarrassed silence until Peter blurted out what everyone else was thinking: "Lord, do you wash my feet?" (v. 6). The question holds more theology than Peter realized. What kind of lord kneels before his servants?

Jesus answered with patience: "What I am doing you do not understand now, but afterward you will understand." The word "afterward" points beyond the supper to the cross and resurrection, when love's logic would finally make sense. But Peter, impulsive as ever, refused—"You shall never wash my feet!" (v. 8). In that protest is the instinct of pride: he couldn't accept grace that reversed hierarchy. Jesus responded, "If I do not wash you, you have no share with me." The foot-washing thus moved from example to symbolism. It represented the cleansing only Jesus can provide.

Peter overcorrected, asking for a full bath. Jesus clarified: "The one who has bathed does not need to wash, except for his feet, but is completely clean. And you are clean, but not every one of you" (v. 10). Daily defilement still needs daily cleansing, but the fundamental washing of salvation has already occurred. John inserts the note: "For he knew who was to betray him." Judas's unwashed soul stands in contrast to the purified hearts of true disciples. Service without surrender is hollow; contact with Jesus does not guarantee cleansing.

The pattern of the towel (13:12–20)

When Jesus finished, he put on his garments and resumed his place. The visual sermon was complete, and now he interpreted it: "Do you understand what I have done to you?" (v. 12). They called him Teacher and Lord—and rightly so—but those titles meant something different now. Authority, in Jesus' kingdom, expresses itself through humility. "If I then, your Lord and Teacher, have washed your feet, you also ought to wash one another's feet" (v. 14).

This is not merely about literal foot-washing, though the act itself may be repeated. It is a mandate for the entire posture of discipleship. The verbs "ought to" and "have given you an example" indicate an enduring moral pattern: those who have received divine cleansing must embody divine service. The servant is not greater than his master (v. 16); therefore, there can be no hierarchy of dignity in the community of the washed.

In verse 17 Jesus added a beatitude: "If you know these things, blessed are you if you do them." Knowledge without imitation is sterile. The world measures greatness by command; Jesus measures it by compassion. The towel, not the throne, defines glory.

Yet this moment of tender instruction carried a shadow. Jesus warned that not all who ate bread with him were blessed; Scripture had to be fulfilled: "He who ate my bread has lifted his heel against me" (v. 18, quoting Psa. 41:9). Even betrayal couldn't thwart the plan—it authenticated it. Jesus sent the disciples out as witnesses: "Whoever receives the one I send receives me" (v. 20). The mission of the church, then, extends the basin and towel to the world. Servants wash because they have been washed; they forgive because they have been forgiven.

The darkness of betrayal (13:21–30)

The mood shifts. John writes, "After saying these things, Jesus was troubled in his spirit" (v. 21). The verb "troubled" echoes earlier scenes (11:33; 12:27). The servant who washed dirty feet now faced the grime of betrayal. He declares openly, "Truly, truly, I say to you, one of you will betray me." The disciples looked at one another, uncertain whom he meant. The intimacy of the table suddenly felt like tension.

Leaning against Jesus' chest was the beloved disciple, a symbol of faith's nearness. Peter signaled him to ask who it was. Jesus answered, "It is he to whom I will give this morsel of bread when I have dipped it" (v. 26). In that culture, offering a dipped morsel was an act of honor—a final gesture of friendship. Even here, grace reached out. Judas received the morsel, and immediately "Satan entered into him."

Jesus said, "What you are going to do, do quickly." None of the others understood; they assumed Judas was handling funds for the feast or giving to the poor. But John's narration is stark: "So, after receiving the morsel of bread, he immediately went out. And it was night" (v. 30). Darkness closed in—not merely physical night but moral night. The contrast between light and darkness, belief and unbelief, now took human form. The light of the world knelt; one of his own walked away.

The new commandment of glory (13:31–35)

Only after Judas departed did Jesus speak of glory: "Now is the Son of Man glorified, and God is glorified in him" (v. 31). The cross, which appeared shameful to human eyes, was heaven's revelation of divine beauty. Glory in

John's Gospel is not a shimmer of gold but the radiance of self-giving love. The mutual glorification of Father and Son demonstrates that the essence of God is not power hoarded but love poured out.

Then Jesus turned to his remaining disciples with intimate address: "Little children, yet a little while I am with you" (v. 33). He was preparing them for absence by giving them the presence of a command that would sustain community: "A new commandment I give to you, that you love one another: just as I have loved you, you also are to love one another" (v. 34).

What was new about it? Love itself is not novel; Leviticus 19:18 already commanded it. The newness lay in the measure ("as I have loved you"), the model (the servant's example), and the mission ("by this all people will know that you are my disciples"). The church's evangelism begins with its ethic. When Christians mirror the self-giving love of Christ, they become the visible continuation of his glory. Foot-washing becomes not a relic of ritual but a rhythm of life.

In a world that idolizes dominance, Jesus inaugurated a community that conquers through compassion. Mutual love is not sentimental tolerance but cruciform commitment—the willingness to stoop, forgive, and serve even the unworthy. The basin and the commandment are two halves of the same gospel.

The limits of zeal (13:36–38)

Peter, never content with silence, asked, "Lord, where are you going?" Jesus replied, "Where I am going you cannot follow now, but you will follow afterward" (v. 36). As before, Peter missed the timing. He wanted to prove his devotion immediately: "I will lay down my life for you." The words sound noble, but Jesus answered with piercing realism: "Will you lay down your life for me? Truly, truly, I say to you, the rooster will not crow till you have denied me three times."

Peter's zeal was genuine yet fragile. His love lacked the endurance that only the Spirit would later supply. The chapter ends as it began—with love misunderstood. Judas betrayed, and Peter boasted; both failed. Between them stood Jesus, steady in purpose, unwavering in love.

John 13 exposes the gap between human intention and divine compassion. It reminds the reader that salvation does not depend on our loyalty but on his. The glory of the chapter lies not in the disciples' devotion but in the Lord's. He knelt before dirty feet, washed the grime, and called them clean. He commanded what only his cross would make possible: "Love one another, as I have loved you."

The basin anticipated the blood. The towel pointed to the tomb. When glory kneels, grace rises.

APPLICATION

1. Greatness begins with a towel

Jesus redefined glory by kneeling. The act of washing feet isn't a sentimental gesture—it's the blueprint for Christian leadership. True greatness begins where pride ends. The basin and towel are not props of servitude but instruments of love. When we serve without recognition, forgive without applause, or bear another's burden without complaint, we enter the arena of divine glory. The world climbs ladders; Jesus stoops to lift. The kingdom advances not through dominance but through humility. Every act of quiet service—teaching a child, visiting the sick, helping a neighbor—is a reflection of the One who washed feet before dying for souls.

2. Cleansed people cleanse others

Peter's resistance reminds us how hard it is to receive grace. We prefer to earn rather than be washed. Yet discipleship begins not with what we do for Christ but with what Christ does for us. Only the cleansed can cleanse others. If our hearts are still unwashed—clogged with pride, resentment, or self-sufficiency—we will have nothing life-giving to share. The church is most persuasive when it is most purified. Confession, repentance, and forgiveness are not rituals of shame but rivers of renewal. To serve like Jesus, we must first be washed by Jesus.

3. Love is the new apologetic

Jesus said the world would know his disciples by their love. Arguments can be refuted; affection cannot. The credibility of the gospel rests less on polished sermons and more on communities that embody cruciform love. This love is not niceness—it's the willingness to sacrifice, to serve, to forgive seventy times seven. When believers care for one another across social, racial, and generational lines, the watching world glimpses God. Evangelism begins in how we treat each other. The basin and towel are apologetic tools; through them, glory becomes visible.

4. Faith that fails is not finished

Judas betrayed; Peter denied. Both fell—but only one returned. Peter's story assures us that failure is not final when grace is near. Jesus knew Peter's weakness and still called him "clean." The same Lord who predicts our stumbles also provides our restoration. Faith may falter under pressure, but it can be rekindled by love. When glory kneels, even broken disciples are given another chance. The call is not to perfection but to perseverance—to rise again, washed, forgiven, and sent back into service with towel in hand.

CONCLUSION

The basin and towel are not symbols of weakness but of divine strength. In a world obsessed with climbing higher, Jesus chose to kneel lower. The cross was not a tragic end to his ministry—it was its truest expression. Glory does not glitter; it glows quietly in acts of love that no one else wants to do.

When Jesus rose from that floor, he left a pattern for every disciple: the way up is down, the way to lead is to serve, the way to love is to stoop. In the kingdom of God, the towel always outshines the throne.

REFLECTION

1. What does it mean that Jesus "loved them to the end"?
2. How does Jesus' humility redefine your understanding of glory?
3. Why do we often resist receiving grace, like Peter did?
4. In what ways has Jesus washed your "feet" this week?
5. How is love the truest evidence of belief?
6. What part of your life still needs cleansing by Christ's humility?

DISCUSSION

7. How does foot-washing reveal the heart of discipleship?
8. What modern "towel" acts can display Christ-like love today?
9. Why is mutual service essential for church unity?
10. How can believers love one another "as Jesus loved"?
11. What distinguishes Peter's failure from Judas's betrayal?
12. How does glory look different in God's kingdom than in ours?

2

THE WAY HOME

JOHN 14

Objective: To show that Jesus himself is our way, peace, and promise of eternal presence.

INTRODUCTION

A few years ago, a pilot described what it feels like to fly through thick fog using only instruments. "You can't trust your senses," he said. "Your body tells you the plane is upside down when it isn't. You have to trust what you can't see—the instruments never lie." That's what faith looks like when the sky goes gray. You keep flying by faith, not sight.

The disciples in John 14 were in that same fog. Their teacher had spoken of leaving, betrayal, denial, and death. The man who had walked on water now talked about walking away. Panic settled in. Into that fear, Jesus spoke steady words: "Let not your hearts be troubled. Believe in God; believe also in me."

John 14 is not a theological lecture; it's a lifeline. Jesus doesn't hand them a map—he gives them himself. He doesn't promise an easier route—he promises a prepared place. He doesn't remove their fear—he replaces it with faith.

In this chapter, the road home is marked by trust, guided by the Spirit, and sealed with peace. The One who is the way doesn't just show us where to go—he walks with us every step of the journey.

EXAMINATION

Comfort for troubled hearts (14:1–4)

The upper room had grown heavy with confusion. Jesus had just predicted betrayal, announced his departure, and foretold Peter's denial. The disciples' confidence, built over three years of following him, collapsed in a moment. Into that silence, Jesus spoke the most compassionate imperative in the Gospel: "Let not your hearts be troubled" (v. 1). The Greek phrasing suggests, "Stop being troubled and do not let it continue." He offers a command that only grace can enable.

Faith is the antidote to anxiety: "Believe in God; believe also in me." The parallel construction equates trust in Jesus with trust in the Father. The cure for panic is not information but relationship. What Jesus asked of them was not so much greater courage as it was deeper confidence.

He then reframed their loss in terms of homecoming. "In my Father's house are many rooms… I go to prepare a place for you" (v. 2). The "Father's house" is not a celestial subdivision but a metaphor for eternal fellowship. The "rooms" (Greek *monai*) suggest abiding places, not mansions—echoing the same verb that will appear later when Jesus speaks of abiding in him (15:4). Heaven is not defined by architecture but by presence.

Jesus' departure was not abandonment; it was preparation. His going (through death and resurrection) ensured their coming. The cross would not be the end of companionship but the beginning of communion. The disciples feared being left behind, but Jesus assured them they were being led home. "Where I am you may be also" (v. 3). The heart of heaven is Jesus himself.

The way, the truth, and the life (14:5–7)

Thomas voiced what the rest dared not: "Lord, we do not know where you are going. How can we know the way?" (v. 5). His honesty earned one of Jesus' most sweeping declarations: "I am the way, and the truth, and the life. No one comes to the Father except through me" (v. 6).

Each term unfolds the nature of divine revelation. Jesus does not merely point to a road; he is the road. He is not a teacher of truth; he embodies truth. He does not offer life as a commodity; he is life itself. The definite article before each term—*the* way, *the* truth, *the* life—excludes all rivals.

"The way" is primary, explaining how "truth" and "life" find expression. Because he is the revelation of truth and the giver of life, he alone grants access to the Father. This is not arrogance but reality. There is no valid knowledge of God apart from Christ. The exclusivity of Jesus is not exclusionary pride—it is the invitation of divine certainty.

He continues, "If you had known me, you would have known my Father also. From now on you do know him and have seen him" (v. 7). The incarnation ends humanity's groping for God in the dark. To see Jesus is to see the Father's heart, voice, and hands. Christianity is not so much a map to heaven as communion with the Lord himself.

Seeing the Father (14:8–11)

Philip's request—"Lord, show us the Father, and it is enough for us"—captures humanity's longing for visible assurance. He wanted a Sinai-like vision, some unmistakable proof. Jesus' response carries both tenderness and ache: "Have I been with you so long, and you still do not know me?" (v. 9). His words rebuked ignorance born of intimacy. They had seen countless miracles, yet they still craved spectacle.

"Whoever has seen me has seen the Father." This is the clearest claim of divine identity in the Gospel of John. Jesus is not merely God's representative; he is God's revelation. The works he performed were not demonstrations of power but disclosures of united divinity: "The words that I say to you I do not speak on my own authority, but the Father who dwells in me does his works" (v. 10).

Notice the fusion of word and deed: the Father "dwells" in the Son, just as believers will later "abide" in him. Jesus' miracles are the Father's fingerprints. His compassion is the Father's heart made visible. When Jesus touched lepers, forgave sinners, and calmed storms, the unseen God was showing his face.

Faith, then, is not blind belief but recognition. Jesus invited his disciples to trust both his words and his works. If they could not yet grasp theology, they could at least follow the evidence of love. The glory of God no longer dwelt behind a veil but walked among them with a towel and a cross.

Greater works and prayer (14:12–14)

Jesus now pivoted from revelation to participation: "Truly, truly, I say to you, whoever believes in me will also do the works that I do; and greater works than these will he do, because I am going to the Father" (v. 12).

"Greater" does not mean more miraculous but more expansive. The disciples would not outshine Jesus in power but extend his mission in scope. Through the Spirit, their ministry would reach beyond the borders of Palestine to the ends of the earth. The resurrection would transform their fear into faith, and their witness would bring life to multitudes. When Peter preached at Pentecost, more were converted in one day than during Jesus' three-year ministry.

These "greater works" flow from prayer: "Whatever you ask in my name, this I will do, that the Father may be glorified in the Son" (v. 13). Prayer "in my name" is not a formula but alignment—asking in harmony with Jesus' character and purpose. The goal is not our success but the Father's glory.

Jesus' promise, "If you ask me anything in my name, I will do it," (v. 14) united divine sovereignty and human petition. The church's mission advances when disciples depend on the presence of an unseen but active Lord. Our future effectiveness rests not on our eloquence but on his ongoing work through prayerful faith.

The promise of the Spirit (14:15–26)

If the disciples feared losing Jesus' presence, his next promise dismantled that fear. "If you love me, you will keep my commandments. And I will ask the Father, and he will give you another Helper, to be with you forever" (vv. 15–16).

The word Helper (*paraklētos*) can mean "advocate," "comforter," or "counselor." Jesus was the first Paraclete; the Spirit is "another of the same kind." The Spirit's coming ensured that Jesus' departure was not loss but multiplication. No longer bound to one body in one place, Christ would dwell within his followers through the Spirit's presence.

The Spirit is called "the Spirit of truth," who "dwells with you and will be in you" (v. 17). The world cannot receive him because it refuses the truth he reveals. The Spirit's indwelling transforms disciples from students into participants. They will not merely recall Jesus' words; they will live them.

In verse 18, Jesus gives one of the most intimate promises of the Gospel: "I will not leave you as orphans; I will come to you." His coming refers both to the resurrection and the ongoing ministry of the Spirit. Through this indwelling presence, Christians experience a living communion that transcends physical sight.

Verses 21–24 trace a circle of mutual love: those who love Jesus obey his word, and those who obey in turn experience the Father's love and indwelling. The divine life becomes relational, not ritual. The Father, Son, and Spirit make their home (Greek *monēn*) within the believer—the same word translated "rooms" in verse 2. The "many rooms" of heaven begin now in the heart inhabited by God.

The Spirit's role as teacher and reminder (v. 26) secured the reliability of apostolic witness. He would "teach you all things and bring to your remembrance all that I have said to you." This was not a promise of fresh revelation for every generation but of faithful preservation for the first. The Spirit ensured that what Jesus said was remembered, understood, and recorded for all who believe.

Peace for the road ahead (14:27–31)

The chapter closes as it began—with comfort. "Peace I leave with you; my peace I give to you" (v. 27). The Hebrew background of *shalom* signifies more than the absence of conflict. It means wholeness, reconciliation, and flourishing under God's rule. The world offers peace through distraction or domination; Jesus offers peace through reconciliation and relationship.

His peace is both gift and presence. It is not earned but bestowed. It does not depend on circumstances but on connection. "Not as the world gives do I give to you." The world promises relief; Jesus provides restoration.

Again, he repeated: "Let not your hearts be troubled, neither let them be afraid" (v. 27). The same love that stooped with a towel now steadied trembling hearts. The disciples would soon see him arrested and crucified, yet even then, he wanted them to interpret those events as victory, not defeat.

Jesus spoke of the ruler of this world coming (v. 30). Satan's approach was real, but his reign is doomed. The cross would look like conquest for evil but was, in truth, its undoing. "He has no claim on me," Jesus said—literally, "He has nothing in me." The purity of the Son secures the peace of his people.

The final verse prepared them to leave the upper room: "Rise, let us go from here" (v. 31). The words were both practical and prophetic. The conversation would continue on the way to Gethsemane, but the decision had been made. Jesus would walk the path home so his followers could find the way there. The peace he gives is not escape from the world but courage to face it.

John 14 begins with troubled hearts and ends with trusting hearts. Between them stood the way, the truth, and the life. The one who left prepares the place. The one who departed sent the Spirit. The One who died brought peace. The journey home has already begun.

APPLICATION

1. Faith is the antidote to fear

The first command of John 14 is not "understand" but "believe." Anxiety fades not so much through answers as through trust. Jesus calls us to anchor confidence in his character, not in our circumstances. We cannot control tomorrow, but we can cling to the one who already stands there. When faith replaces fear, obedience follows naturally. The heart at rest is not empty—it is full of Christ. Every believer faces seasons of confusion, yet the same Jesus who calmed the sea still whispers, "Let not your heart be troubled."

2. Salvation is personal, not positional

Thomas wanted directions; Jesus offered himself. Christianity is not about finding a better route but following a living Savior. "I am the way" means that access to God is relational, not ritual. We do not ascend to heaven by performance but by abiding in Christ. The greatest tragedy is to know about the path and never walk it. Our world prizes autonomy, but the gospel invites surrender. The way home is not discovered through achievement; it's received through attachment. To walk with Jesus is to arrive even before we see the destination.

3. The Spirit makes absence impossible

When Jesus promised the Spirit, he replaced despair with indwelling. What seemed like abandonment became expansion. The Spirit transforms Christians into walking temples—mobile sanctuaries of divine presence. Through him, Jesus' voice still teaches, convicts, comforts, and reminds. The same Spirit who hovered over creation now inhabits the redeemed.

This means we never pray into emptiness or serve in isolation. Our Helper doesn't merely visit; he resides. The Spirit's role is not to entertain the church but to empower it—to make Christ's presence real wherever we are. The way home is traveled with heaven already living inside us.

4. Peace is the signature of belief

The farewell gift of Jesus is peace—not the fragile calm the world sells, but the deep assurance the cross secures. Peace is not the absence of storms but the settled confidence that God reigns within them. The Christian's heart can be still even when life shakes violently, because Christ's victory has already silenced the accuser. When fear rises, we remember: the tomb is empty, the Spirit is present, and the future is secure. The way home is paved with peace, not panic. Those who know Jesus can rest while the world trembles, for the Prince of Peace has already spoken, "It is finished."

CONCLUSION

The road home is not a mystery to solve but a person to trust. Jesus does not hand out directions; he offers himself. Every fear the disciples felt that night still visits our hearts today—loss, uncertainty, separation—but his words remain: "Let not your hearts be troubled." The same Savior who prepares a place is preparing his people. The Spirit ensures that absence will never mean abandonment, and his peace still quiets restless souls.

Yet Jesus' comfort does more than steady troubled hearts—it calls them to deeper connection. As the journey continues, Jesus will speak of abiding, of remaining in him as branches in a vine. The way home becomes a way of life. Lesson 3 begins there—with the secret of staying close to the One who never leaves.

REFLECTION

1. What does Jesus' command "Let not your hearts be troubled" reveal about faith?
2. How does believing in Jesus comfort fear better than understanding circumstances?
3. In what ways does Jesus' "I am" statement shape your daily trust?
4. How does the Spirit's presence change your sense of loneliness or purpose?
5. What kind of peace has Jesus given you recently?
6. How can obedience deepen your awareness of God's indwelling presence?

DISCUSSION

1. Why is heaven described as a prepared place for prepared people?
2. What makes Jesus' claim, "I am the way," both exclusive and inviting?
3. How are "greater works" possible for ordinary disciples today?
4. What role does the Spirit play in your understanding of Scripture?
5. How does Jesus' peace differ from worldly comfort or control?
6. Where do you see "troubled hearts" today that need this chapter's hope?

3

ABIDE IN ME

JOHN 15:1-17

Objective: To show that abiding in Christ produces lasting fruit through love, obedience, and divine friendship.

INTRODUCTION

A vineyard is a noisy place in spring. Pruners move row by row, shears clicking rhythmically as they cut away excess growth. To the untrained eye, the vine looks butchered—bare, even lifeless. But to the vintner, every cut is calculated. He knows where fruit will grow and what must be removed so the vine can flourish. The sound of pruning is the sound of preparation.

When Jesus and his disciples left the upper room, they likely passed through such vineyards on their way to Gethsemane. Against that backdrop, Jesus said, "I am the true vine, and my Father is the vinedresser." The metaphor was familiar—Israel had long been called God's vine—but now Jesus declared himself the faithful one, the source of all true life and fruitfulness.

In John 15, the conversation turns from comfort to connection. The peace Jesus promised in chapter 14 now became participation in his life. Abiding is not clinging in fear but remaining in love. The Father tends, the Son supplies, and the Spirit sustains. To be a disciple is to draw our life from his.

The vineyard belongs to the Gardener; the branches belong to the Vine. And every fruitful life begins with one invitation: "Abide in me."

EXAMINATION

The true vine and the vinedresser (15:1–3)

The upper room conversation continued, and the imagery now turned agricultural. Jesus said, "I am the true vine, and my Father is the vinedresser" (v. 1). This is the seventh and final "I am" statement in John's Gospel, and it carries the weight of culmination. In the Old Testament, Israel was often described as God's vine (Psa. 80; Isa. 5:1–7; Hos. 10:1–2), yet always as a disappointing one—luxuriant in leaves, barren in fruit. By calling himself the true vine, Jesus identified himself as the faithful Israel, the embodiment of all that God's people were meant to be.

The Father tends this vine as the expert gardener. He "takes away" branches that bear no fruit and "prunes" those that do, that they may bear more. The verb for "prune" (*kathairō*) means both to cleanse and to trim. Pruning, though painful, is purposeful. The Father removes whatever impedes growth—sin, self-sufficiency, distraction—so that life can flourish.

Jesus added, "Already you are clean because of the word that I have spoken to you" (v. 3). The same Word that called Lazarus from the tomb and washed Peter's feet now purified the disciples' hearts. The pruning knife of the Word may sting (Heb. 4:12), but it never wounds without healing. Fruitfulness begins with cleansing, and cleansing comes through submission to Jesus' Word. The first step in abiding is allowing the Gardener to cut away what cannot bear fruit.

Abiding and fruitfulness (15:4–6)

"Abide in me, and I in you." The command and the promise are intertwined. Abiding is not a momentary visit but a continual dwelling—remaining, depending, enduring. The Greek verb *menō* ("abide," "dwell") appears eleven times in this chapter, forming its heartbeat. The relationship Jesus describes is not mechanical but organic. Disciples are not employees performing duties but branches drawing life from the vine.

Just as a branch cannot bear fruit by itself, so we cannot produce anything lasting apart from Christ. Busyness is not fruitfulness; activity is not abiding. Churches may appear green with leaves—programs, numbers, events—yet without the sap of the vine, there is no real growth. Jesus' warning is clear: "Apart from me you can do nothing" (v. 5). The word "nothing" leaves no exceptions. The greatest sermons, hymns, or ministries become lifeless twigs without the living connection of faith.

Verse 6 sobers us further: "If anyone does not abide in me, he is thrown away like a branch and withers; and the branches are gathered, thrown into the fire, and burned." The image recalls Judas—a man connected externally but not internally. The withered branch represents profession without participation. The fire symbolizes divine judgment, not against temporary weakness but against total separation. The contrast is poignant: abide and bear fruit, or detach and wither. The difference between the two is not effort but intimacy.

The fruit of prayer and glory (15:7–8)

Jesus now connected abiding to prayer: "If you abide in me, and my words abide in you, ask whatever you wish, and it will be done for you" (v. 7). This is not a blank check for indulgence but a covenantal promise for those who dwell in alignment with his will. When Jesus' words saturate our hearts, our desires begin to echo his own. Prayer then becomes less about convincing God and more about cooperating with him.

Fruitfulness, prayer, and glory form a chain: "By this my Father is glorified, that you bear much fruit and so prove to be my disciples" (v. 8). Fruit-bearing glorifies the Father because it mirrors his character in the Son. The gardener delights in seeing his vine heavy with clusters. This is discipleship's ultimate purpose—not personal fulfillment or visible success, but the Father's honor.

The fruit itself includes both inward character and outward witness. Love, joy, peace, patience—these are the grapes of the Spirit (Gal. 5:22–23). But fruit also multiplies in the harvest of souls, as disciples reproduce disciples. When God's people abide deeply, their lives display his beauty publicly. True spirituality is never sterile; it blossoms into blessing.

Abiding in love (15:9–11)

"As the Father has loved me, so have I loved you. Abide in my love" (v. 9). The vine metaphor expands into a love story. The same love that flows between Father and Son now flows into the branches. Discipleship, then, is participation in divine affection. Jesus does not merely command love; he invites believers to remain within its current.

To abide in love means to rest, trust, and stay in the orbit of grace. Yet love is not a vague feeling—it has a tangible form: obedience. "If you keep my commandments, you will abide in my love, just as I have kept my Father's commandments and abide in his love" (v. 10). The pattern is relational, not mechanical. Obedience is how love breathes; it is affection translated into action.

Jesus' goal is joy, not drudgery: "These things I have spoken to you, that my joy may be in you, and that your joy may be full" (v. 11). The joy of Jesus is not circumstantial happiness but the settled delight of doing the Father's will. The branch that abides discovers joy not by avoiding pruning but by yielding to it. When we live in step with his love, joy ceases to be fragile—it becomes our native atmosphere.

Friendship through obedience and sacrifice (15:12–15)

Jesus moved from the metaphor of vine and branches to the intimacy of friendship. "This is my commandment, that you love one another as I have loved you" (v. 12). The word "as" (*kathōs*) carries both comparison and cause—we love because, and as, Christ has loved us. The standard of Christian love is no longer self-interest or reciprocity but cruciform imitation.

Verse 13 marks the summit of the discourse: "Greater love has no one than this, that someone lay down his life for his friends." The cross defines friendship in divine terms. In ancient culture, friendship implied loyalty, shared purpose, and mutual disclosure. Jesus redefines it through sacrifice. His death would not only save sinners but also transform servants into companions.

He explained, "You are my friends if you do what I command you" (v. 14). This is not conditional affection but covenant participation. Friendship with Jesus is a shared mission. Obedience is not the price of love but its proof. Then comes the astonishing shift: "No longer do I call you servants… but I have called you friends, for all that I have heard from my Father I have made known to you" (v. 15). Jesus drew his disciples into the circle of divine intimacy, revealing not only commands but also the heart behind them. The Creator of the universe called them friends.

Every command from his lips is therefore an act of inclusion, not exclusion. To follow him is to walk alongside him. To keep his word is to know his heart. The vine and branches are not cold conduits of life—they are the living union of friendship.

Chosen and appointed to bear fruit (15:16–17)

The discourse ends where it began—with divine initiative and abiding love. "You did not choose me, but I chose you and appointed you that you should go and bear fruit and that your fruit should abide" (v. 16). The language echoes the commissioning of Israel in the Old Testament and reframes it around Jesus' mission. The disciples did not stumble into friendship by luck; they were selected by grace. The verb "appointed" implies purpose and permanence.

The phrase "go and bear fruit" combines movement and growth. Abiding is not passivity—it propels mission. To remain in Christ does not mean retreat from the world but engagement with it. The fruit that abides (*menē*) connects back to the central verb of the chapter; lasting fruit arises only from lasting fellowship. Evangelism without abiding is activism; abiding without outreach is inertia.

Jesus repeated the promise: "Whatever you ask the Father in my name, he may give it to you." Prayer again appears as the vine's circulatory system, channeling divine life into human need. Effective prayer flows from chosen identity and obedient intimacy.

The section concludes with the refrain: "These things I command you, so that you will love one another" (v. 17). Love remains the test and testimony of all true discipleship. The pruning knife, the abiding branch, the fruitful life—all converge on love. The Christian life begins in the Father's choosing, continues in the Son's friendship, and thrives through the Spirit's indwelling.

In the end, the picture is simple yet inexhaustible: Jesus is the true vine, the Father the wise gardener, and believers the living branches. Pruned but alive, we exist to bear the fruit of love that endures forever. Abiding ought to be less an obligation to meet and more a relationship to enjoy. To remain in him is to live as we were always meant to—rooted, nourished, fruitful, and free.

APPLICATION

1. Pruning is proof of the Father's care

Pruning hurts, but it's not punishment—it's proof that we belong to the Gardener. God trims not to harm but to heal, cutting away habits, attitudes, and attachments that choke spiritual growth. Every snip of the blade is aimed at greater fruitfulness. When we experience loss or correction, we can trust that the Father's hands are steady and skilled. The pain of pruning often precedes the joy of harvest. A branch left untouched eventually grows wild and weak; a pruned branch becomes strong and productive. The Father's discipline isn't a sign of rejection but of relationship. If he's pruning, he's preparing you to bear more.

2. Abiding is a daily dependence

To abide in Christ is to breathe his life continually, not occasionally. It's not a one-time decision at baptism but an everyday posture of reliance. We remain connected through prayer, Scripture, worship, and obedience—the conduits through which his life flows into ours. The Christian who abides doesn't manufacture fruit but manifests it naturally. Staying close to Jesus keeps our hearts nourished and our witness fresh. Separation breeds dryness; dependence breeds delight. Abiding means we no longer strive to earn love—we rest in it. Spiritual vitality doesn't come from effort alone but from union with the vine who never withers.

3. Friendship with Jesus changes everything

The King of heaven calls us friends, not merely followers. That truth dismantles both pride and despair. We are not servants scrambling for approval but companions entrusted with God's heart. Friendship with Jesus means shared purpose and honest obedience. He invites us into divine confidence—knowing his will and carrying it out in the world. Such friendship is maintained through listening and loving, not through status or merit. The closer we walk with him, the more we resemble him. Friendship with Christ transforms duty into delight and commands into conversations. When we know his friendship, obedience becomes joy, not obligation.

4. Love is the only lasting fruit

At the end of every command, illustration, and metaphor in this passage stands one word: love. Every sermon, prayer, and act of service that does not produce love is fruitless. The measure of discipleship isn't how much we know but how much we love. Jesus' kind of love is self-giving, enduring, and practical. It stoops like a servant and sacrifices like a friend. This love can't be imitated apart from abiding—it's the natural yield of a life connected to Christ. Programs and productivity fade, but love abides. When our hearts overflow with his love, the world tastes something it can't find anywhere else: the fruit of heaven growing on earthly branches.

CONCLUSION

Abiding in Christ is not a mystical secret—it's the daily rhythm of love and trust. The Father prunes, the Son sustains, and the Spirit supplies. Our only task is to remain connected. Fruitfulness is not forced; it's the inevitable result of fellowship. When we abide, the life of Christ flows freely through us, shaping our character and strengthening our witness.

Yet the vineyard is not an oasis cut off from the world. In the next lesson, Jesus prepares his disciples for what comes when the world rejects that fruit. The vine will face the storm. Lesson 4 will show us how abiding love endures amid the world's hatred.

REFLECTION

1. What does pruning reveal about God's care and your spiritual growth?
2. How do you daily remain connected to Christ, the true vine?
3. What habits or attitudes hinder your fruitfulness in him?
4. How has friendship with Jesus reshaped your view of obedience?
5. Where have you seen his love produce lasting fruit in your life?
6. What does abiding look like when life feels dry or difficult?

DISCUSSION

1. Why is Jesus called the true vine in contrast to Israel?
2. How can pruning strengthen rather than discourage believers?
3. What does "apart from me you can do nothing" mean practically?
4. How does abiding affect our prayers and our service?
5. What makes love the defining evidence of discipleship?
6. How can the church embody friendship with Jesus together?

4

HELP IN THE HEAT OF HOSTILITY

JOHN 15:18–16:15

Objective: To show how the Spirit empowers Christians to endure hatred and glorify Christ.

INTRODUCTION

During the Second World War, a small French village hid dozens of Jewish families from Nazi patrols. One night, soldiers surrounded the town. A terrified boy asked the local minister, "What will happen if they find us?" The minister replied quietly, "Then we will tell the truth." The boy frowned. "And what will happen if they kill us?" The pastor smiled sadly. "Then we will still tell the truth."

Courage doesn't mean the absence of fear—it means choosing truth over comfort. That is the heartbeat of John 15:18–16:15. After describing the beauty of abiding love, Jesus prepared his disciples for the world's reaction to that love. Fruitful branches will face pruning not only from the Father's hand but also from the world's hostility.

Yet the same Jesus who warned of hatred also promised help. The Holy Spirit would come—not to spare them from persecution, but to strengthen them through it. The Advocate would give courage to their hearts and clarity to their words.

In this lesson, we learn that the church's mission has always existed between two realities: the world's opposition and the Spirit's empowerment. The vine will face the storm—but the life within it will never die.

EXAMINATION

The world's hatred (15:18–25)

The sweetness of the vineyard gives way to the chill of opposition. Jesus, who had just spoken of abiding in love, now warned of abiding in conflict: "If the world hates you, know that it has hated me before it hated you" (v. 18). The love of the vine does not exempt the branches from hostility—it guarantees it. The disciples were about to learn that fruit-bearing faith attracts both hunger and hatred.

The term "world" (*kosmos*) here refers not to the physical creation but to the human system organized against God—society in rebellion. It is the realm of unbelief, where darkness resists the light. The world's hatred is not accidental; it is theological. Jesus said, "If you were of the world, the world would love you as its own; but because you are not of the world… therefore the world hates you" (v. 19). The more our lives reflect his character, the more the world's hostility toward him will transfer to us.

This is not an argument for isolation or paranoia but for realism. Following Christ means inheriting both his mission and his opposition. The servant is not greater than the master (v. 20). If they persecuted him, they will persecute his followers. Their reaction exposes their true knowledge—or lack thereof—of God. "They will do these things because they have not known the Father, nor me" (v. 21).

Persecution, then, becomes diagnostic. The world's hatred is evidence that the message of Jesus still confronts human pride. Light exposes darkness, and darkness resists exposure. Yet even this resistance fulfills Scripture: "They hated me without a cause" (v. 25, quoting Psa. 35:19; 69:4). Jesus is the innocent sufferer of the Psalms, the righteous one rejected by those he came to save. In this section, Jesus redefines suffering as participation in his story. The hatred of the world is not proof of failure but of fidelity. The vineyard will bear fruit, but not without frost.

The witness of the Spirit (15:26–27)

Jesus shifted from warning to reassurance. "But when the Helper comes, whom I will send to you from the Father, the Spirit of truth, who proceeds from the Father, he will bear witness about me" (v. 26). The "Helper" (*Paraklētos*) is the same Spirit promised in chapter 14—a term rich with meaning: comforter, counselor, advocate, defender.

The Spirit's first ministry is testimony. He continues the witness of Jesus by declaring the truth of the Son to a hostile world. While the world rejects Christ, the Spirit reveals him. While hatred silences voices, the Spirit empowers them. This verse unfolds a Trinitarian pattern: the Father sends the Spirit through the Son to bear witness about the Son.

Yet this witness is not solitary: "And you also will bear witness, because you have been with me from the beginning" (v. 27). The Spirit did not replace the disciples' testimony; he enabled it. Together, divine and human witness join to convict and invite the world. The gospel is not advanced by clever rhetoric but by Spirit-powered testimony.

Every Christian thus becomes part of a cosmic courtroom. The world prosecutes Christ; the Spirit defends him through our words and lives. The church's mission stands or falls not on cultural favor but on faithfulness to testify. The same Spirit who descended at Pentecost still equips ordinary people to speak extraordinary truth.

Preparation for persecution (16:1–7)

"I have said all these things to you to keep you from falling away." (16:1). Jesus' goal was not to frighten but to fortify. The Greek term *skandalizō* ("fall away") evokes the image of tripping over an unexpected obstacle. By warning them, Jesus removed the surprise of suffering. Faith stumbles more over shock than pain.

He explained that persecution will come not only from pagan hostility but also from religious zeal. "They will put you out of the synagogues. Indeed, the hour is coming when whoever kills you will think he is offering service to God" (v. 2). The irony is bitter: violence done in the name of God will mark those who least know him. Paul's pre-conversion life illustrates this perfectly—zeal without knowledge becomes cruelty baptized in sincerity.

Jesus framed this forewarning with both compassion and purpose. "I did not say these things to you from the beginning, because I was with you" (v. 4). His physical presence had shielded them from the full force of opposition; his departure would expose them to it. Yet that very departure would inaugurate something greater: "It is to your advantage that I go away, for if I do not go away, the Helper will not come to you" (v. 7).

Here is one of the paradoxes of faith: loss can become gain. The disciples couldn't imagine anything good coming from Jesus' absence, but he insisted it was necessary. The Spirit's coming would transform fear into courage, confusion into clarity, isolation into indwelling. The cross would not end their fellowship—it would expand it.

The Spirit's conviction (16:8–11)

Jesus explained the Spirit's convicting ministry: "And when he comes, he will convict the world concerning sin and righteousness and judgment" (v. 8). The verb *elenchō* means to expose, to cross-examine, or to convince of error. The Spirit acts as a divine prosecutor, presenting the case of heaven against the rebellion of earth.

First, he convicts "concerning sin, because they do not believe in me" (v. 9). The ultimate sin is unbelief—the refusal to trust Jesus as the revelation of God. The Spirit reveals that all moral failure flows from this root. He does not simply make people feel guilty; he awakens them to reality.

Second, the Spirit convicts "concerning righteousness, because I go to the Father, and you will see me no longer" (v. 10). The resurrection and ascension vindicated Jesus as the truly righteous one. The world judged him guilty; the Father declared him innocent. The Spirit continues that vindication in the hearts of Christians, reminding them that righteousness is not human achievement but divine declaration.

Third, the Spirit convicts "concerning judgment, because the ruler of this world is judged" (v. 11). At the cross, Satan's authority was broken. What looked like defeat became victory. The Spirit announces that the trial is over and the verdict rendered. Judgment is not merely future—it has already begun with the overthrow of evil's power.

In these three convictions—sin, righteousness, and judgment—the Spirit exposes humanity's error, vindicates the Son's obedience, and proclaims the devil's defeat. The world's hatred cannot prevail against this threefold witness. Every conversion, every awakening of conscience, is the Spirit's courtroom at work.

The Spirit's guidance and glory (16:12–15)

Jesus closes this section with a final word about the Spirit's role among believers: "I still have many things to say to you, but you cannot bear them now" (v. 12). His compassion recognizes their limits. Revelation must wait for readiness. Truth given too soon can overwhelm rather than edify.

"When the Spirit of truth comes, he will guide you into all the truth" (v. 13). The phrase "all the truth" means the full understanding of what Jesus had already revealed, not new content beyond it. The Spirit's ministry is interpretive, not inventive—he deepens insight into the gospel; he does not add to it. The apostles would later write Scripture under this guidance, ensuring that the church's foundation rested not on speculation but on Spirit-given remembrance.

The Spirit's humility is remarkable: "He will not speak on his own authority, but whatever he hears he will speak" (v. 13). Just as Jesus spoke only what the Father gave him, the Spirit speaks only what the Son gives him. Revelation flows from Father to Son to Spirit to believers—a harmony of divine communication.

Finally, Jesus summarized the Spirit's purpose: "He will glorify me, for he will take what is mine and declare it to you" (v. 14). The Spirit's work is not to draw attention to himself but to magnify Christ. His illumination always leads to adoration. Whenever hearts are drawn to the beauty of Jesus, the Spirit is at work.

Verse 15 ties the circle: "All that the Father has is mine; therefore I said that he will take what is mine and declare it to you." The unity of the Godhead ensures the reliability of revelation. The Spirit communicates the Son's message, which perfectly expresses the Father's mind. To hear the Spirit is to hear the Son; to know the Son is to know the Father.

This section closes the first half of the Farewell Discourse. The world's hatred would intensify, but the Spirit's help would multiply. The disciples' grief would give way to gladness as they discovered that the same Spirit who testified through them also comforted within them.

APPLICATION

1. Expect opposition, not approval

Jesus never promised his followers a comfortable road—only a faithful one.

The world's hatred isn't a sign that we've done something wrong; it's often proof that we're becoming more like him. When our values, ethics, or compassion expose darkness, resistance comes naturally. The goal isn't to court conflict but to remain courageous when it arrives. The servant is not greater than the Master; if they misunderstood him, they'll misunderstand us. Yet persecution refines our character and message. It forces us to depend more deeply on grace and to speak with gentleness rather than resentment. We can endure hostility without our own hostility because we know whom we represent.

2. Speak and serve boldly through the Spirit's power

The same Spirit who descended at Pentecost still empowers timid hearts today. Our task is not to argue the world into belief but to bear truthful, loving witness. The Spirit partners with our words, turning testimony into transformation. Every act of faithfulness—whether sharing the gospel, serving the suffering, or speaking truth in love—is a continuation of the Spirit's work. Courage doesn't come from personality; it comes from presence. When we open our mouths, the Advocate opens hearts. The world may shout down truth, but the Spirit never loses his voice. Wherever Christ is proclaimed, the Spirit is at work defending him.

3. Find comfort in the Spirit's presence

Jesus' departure was not abandonment but advantage. Through the Spirit, his presence became permanent and personal. The Advocate is not a guest who visits on Sundays; he is a resident who abides forever. He convicts, counsels, comforts, and reminds us that we are never alone in a hostile world. When opposition rises, the Spirit steadies trembling hearts and whispers, "You belong to Christ." His ministry is not to remove our trials but to fill them with divine companionship. Every believer has within them the very presence that once walked beside Galilean fishermen. The Helper hasn't retired; he's residing.

4. Let the Spirit glorify Christ in you

The Spirit's greatest work is not in spectacular signs but in daily transformation. He glorifies Jesus by shaping his likeness within us—love in the face of hate, peace amid chaos, and endurance under pressure. The mark of Spirit-filled living is not louder religion but deeper resemblance. As he guided the apostles into truth, he guides us into maturity. Our part is surrender; his part is sanctification. When others see patience, purity, and forgiveness that make no worldly sense, they are glimpsing the glory of Christ. The Spirit's mission hasn't changed—to make Jesus visible in the lives of those who bear his name.

CONCLUSION

Jesus never hid the cost of discipleship. He promised both the world's hatred and the Spirit's help. The cross-shaped life will always meet resistance but never abandonment. The same Spirit who convicts the world also comforts the saints, turning fear into faith and opposition into opportunity. Our task is not to escape hostility but to bear witness within it.

As Jesus moved closer to the cross, his focus shifted from the world's rejection to the disciples' sorrow. In the next lesson, he will speak of grief turning to joy—how loss itself becomes the seed of victory. Lesson 5 will show that sorrow, like pruning, is never the end for those who abide in him.

REFLECTION

1. Why does the world's hatred confirm rather than contradict true discipleship?
2. How can persecution strengthen your dependence on Jesus?
3. When have you sensed the Spirit's help in a difficult situation?
4. How does the Spirit's conviction reveal God's justice and mercy?
5. What does it mean for the Spirit to glorify Christ in you?
6. How can remembering the cross change your view of opposition?

DISCUSSION

1. Why does abiding in Christ provoke the world's hostility?
2. What comfort does the Spirit provide when faith becomes costly?
3. How does the Spirit's conviction differ from human guilt or shame?
4. What does "He will glorify me" teach us about the Spirit's purpose?
5. How can believers testify boldly without becoming combative?
6. What modern examples show the Spirit empowering courageous witness today?

5

THE MORNING AFTER SORROW

JOHN 16:16-33

Objective: To show that Jesus transforms sorrow into lasting joy, prayerful trust, and unshakable peace.

INTRODUCTION

A preacher once compared grief to standing in the doorway of a dark tunnel. "You can't see the other side," he said, "but the wind blowing through tells you there's light ahead." That's how Jesus prepared his disciples in John 16. They were standing at the mouth of the darkest tunnel of their lives, but a breeze of resurrection hope was already whispering through.

Jesus knew the cross would shatter their confidence. In a matter of hours, their teacher would be arrested, condemned, and crucified. The world would celebrate while their hearts would collapse under the weight of despair. Yet in that very moment of loss, God was working redemption. Sorrow would not be replaced *by* joy; it would be transformed *into* joy.

John 16:16–33 brings the Farewell Discourse to a crescendo. Jesus promised that their grief would become gladness, their confusion would give way to prayer, and their fear would yield to peace. The pain of separation would soon give birth to unshakable faith.

Every Christian eventually stands in that same doorway—tasting sorrow, hearing faint whispers of joy. The promise of this passage is, for those who belong to Christ, every tunnel has light at the end because the tomb did, too.

EXAMINATION

A little while (16:16–19)

Jesus had spoken of his departure before, but this time the phrase was puzzling: "A little while, and you will see me no longer; and again a little while, and you will see me" (v. 16). The disciples whispered among themselves, confused. What did he mean by "a little while"? Would he vanish and return in a few days? Was he referring to death, resurrection, or something else entirely?

Their uncertainty mirrors the tension of the cross itself—events were moving faster than faith could process. Jesus' words echo prophetic language from Isaiah, where God promises that suffering will be brief before deliverance arrives (Isa. 26:17–20). The "little while" pointed to the short span between Jesus' death and resurrection, yet the disciples couldn't yet imagine that grief could give birth to glory.

This phrase, "a little while," runs like a thread through the whole passage, tying together time and trust. To human hearts, even a moment of pain feels endless, but in God's economy, sorrow has an expiration date. What they perceived as abandonment would soon prove to be the prelude to victory.

Jesus did not rebuke their confusion; he acknowledged it. Faith often begins not with understanding but with honest bewilderment. The disciples' whispered questions reveal the tension every Christian feels between promise and fulfillment.

Sorrow turned to joy (16:20–22)

Jesus answered their unspoken question with an image that transcends explanation: "Truly, truly, I say to you, you will weep and lament, but the world will rejoice. You will be sorrowful, but your sorrow will turn into joy" (v. 20). Their anguish would coincide with the world's celebration. As his enemies mocked his death, the disciples would mourn—but that mourning would not last.

The transformation was not from sorrow to happiness but from sorrow into joy. The same event—the cross—produces both agony and ecstasy. God would not merely replace their pain; he would redeem it. To make the point vivid, Jesus turned to childbirth: "When a woman is giving birth, she has sorrow because her hour has come, but when she has delivered the baby, she no longer remembers the anguish, for joy that a human being has been born into the world" (v. 21).

This image of labor recalls an earlier "hour"—Jesus' own. His suffering would give birth to new life, not only for himself but for the world. The resurrection would transform the tomb into a delivery room. Pain is not wasted; it becomes the process through which God brings forth joy.

In verse 22, Jesus personalized the promise: "So also you have sorrow now, but I will see you again, and your hearts will rejoice, and no one will take your joy from you." The phrase "I will see you again" reversed their question from verse 16. They wondered, "When will we see you?"—but Jesus answered, "I will see you." Their future depended not on their ability to find him but on his commitment to find them.

This joy is secure because it is anchored in resurrection reality. Earthly happiness depends on changing circumstances; resurrection joy depends on a risen Lord. Once they saw him alive, no threat could ever erase that memory. Their faith would no longer rest on fragile emotion but on unbreakable evidence.

Prayer and understanding (16:23–28)

The next promise deepened their joy by granting them direct access to the Father. "In that day you will ask nothing of me. Truly, truly, I say to you, whatever you ask of the Father in my name, he will give it to you" (v. 23).

"In that day" refers to the post-resurrection era when the Spirit would teach and empower them. Their questions would fade, not because mysteries vanished, but because presence returned. They would understand that the Son's mission had accomplished full reconciliation. The barrier between heaven and earth was removed; prayer no longer required an intermediary other than Jesus himself.

Asking "in my name" is not a formula for wish fulfillment but a relational posture. To pray in his name is to align with his purposes, to speak with his authority, and to rest in his merit. It means praying as those united to him—branches asking the Gardener through the Vine.

Jesus adds a breathtaking assurance: "The Father himself loves you, because you have loved me and have believed that I came from God" (v. 27).

The disciples had no need to fear divine indifference. The same Father who sent the Son now welcomed them with affection. The love once mediated through Jesus is now shared directly through union with him.

Then Jesus summarized his entire mission: "I came from the Father and have come into the world, and now I am leaving the world and going to the Father" (v. 28). These words compress the entire gospel narrative into one sentence—incarnation, revelation, redemption, and return. The disciples' access to God depended entirely on that movement. The Son's departure secured their arrival.

The disciples' misplaced confidence (16:29–32)

For a brief moment, the disciples believed they finally understood. "Ah, now you are speaking plainly and not using figurative speech! Now we know that you know all things… this is why we believe that you came from God" (vv. 29–30).

Their enthusiasm sounds encouraging but reveals premature confidence. They thought knowledge guaranteed strength. Jesus gently corrected them: "Do you now believe? Behold, the hour is coming, indeed it has come, when you will be scattered, each to his own home, and will leave me alone" (v. 31–32).

Their coming failure was not in doubt; their restoration was. Jesus foresaw their collapse but did not revoke their calling. His statement, "Yet I am not alone, for the Father is with me," turned loneliness into assurance. Even abandonment cannot sever the bond between Father and Son.

This section exposes the tension between shallow optimism and genuine faith. The disciples mistook momentary clarity for maturity. Jesus knew that real understanding would only come after the resurrection, when the Spirit turned information into transformation. Until then, they would stumble—but their stumbling would be covered by grace.

There is comfort in Jesus' realism. He knew the weakness of his followers and still called them friends. Our confidence does not rest in our consistency but in his constancy. Even when scattered, the sheep remain his.

Peace in the midst of tribulation (16:33)

The final verse of the chapter stands as both benediction and battle cry: "I have said these things to you, that in me you may have peace. In the world you will have tribulation. But take heart; I have overcome the world."

The statement balances three realities: position, condition, and assurance. **Position:** "In me you may have peace." "Peace" here carries the Hebrew sense of *shalom*—wholeness, harmony, reconciliation. It is not freedom from pressure but fullness within it. **Condition:** "In the world you will have tribulation." The promise of peace coexists with the certainty of pain. Believers are not spared from trouble; they are sustained through it. **Assurance:** "Take heart; I have overcome the world."

The verb "overcome" (*nenikēka*) is in the perfect tense—completed action with ongoing results. The victory is finished, yet its effects continue. Jesus spoke these words before the cross, showing that triumph is not contingent on circumstance but on obedience. The world's hostility, sin's weight, and Satan's schemes have already met their match in him.

This verse closes the Farewell Discourse and prepares for the prayer of John 17. It summarizes the whole message: Peace in him, pressure in the world, victory through the cross. Every Christian life moves within that triangle.

APPLICATION

1. God transforms pain, not just removes it

Jesus didn't promise to erase the disciples' sorrow; he promised to transform it. The same cross that caused their despair became the source of their joy. In God's hands, pain is never wasted—it becomes the soil where joy grows. We often beg God to take away our suffering when he intends to redeem it. The resurrection teaches that joy doesn't arrive after sorrow but through it. Our darkest nights often hide dawn just beyond the horizon. The Christian life is not about avoiding pain but allowing God to turn it into purpose.

2. Prayer is access, not magic

Jesus' promise about asking in his name is an invitation, not a formula. Prayer in his name means praying from within his will and character. The Father loves us and listens, not because we say the right words, but because we belong to his Son. Through prayer, our perspective aligns with heaven's. We don't inform God; we involve him. The disciples would soon learn that prayer is not an escape from trouble but the channel of peace within it. When life feels uncertain, our access to the Father is certain—and that is enough.

3. Confidence without surrender is fragile

The disciples thought understanding equaled maturity—until fear scattered them. Jesus knew their confidence would collapse, yet he loved them still. Knowledge without dependence leads to pride; faith without humility crumbles under pressure. True strength is not the absence of fear but the presence of trust. When we stumble, Jesus' grace gathers us. The same Lord who foresaw their failure restored them by the sea. Our security rests not in our performance but in his perseverance. The lesson of their collapse is mercy: we are upheld by the One we once abandoned.

4. Peace is possible in the middle, not the end

Jesus' final words—"Take heart; I have overcome the world"—redefine peace. It's not the calm after the storm but courage within it. The peace he offers is resurrection peace: victory announced before the battle ends. We live in the tension of "in me" and "in the world"—safe in Christ, yet surrounded by chaos. The key is location, not situation. When our lives are rooted in him, tribulation loses its power to define us. The world shakes, but he stands unshaken. Peace is not the prize at the finish line—it's the presence that runs beside us.

CONCLUSION

The cross turned the disciples' world upside down, but the resurrection turned it right-side up again. Jesus' promise was not empty comfort—it was fulfilled within days. Their weeping became witness, their sorrow became song. That same transformation remains the pattern of discipleship: pain becomes purpose, and despair gives way to peace through Christ's victory.

Yet Jesus' mission is not finished. Before facing the cross, he lifts his eyes and prays—not only for his disciples, but for all who would believe through them. In Lesson 6, we enter the most sacred ground of John's Gospel: the prayer of the Son to the Father on behalf of his own.

REFLECTION

1. When have you seen God turn sorrow into joy in your own life?
2. How does "a little while" shape your patience in suffering?
3. Why is resurrection joy stronger than temporary happiness?
4. What does praying "in Jesus' name" mean for your relationship with the Father?
5. How can peace and tribulation coexist in the believer's life?
6. What helps you "take heart" when the world feels overwhelming?

DISCUSSION

1. What does Jesus' childbirth metaphor teach about pain and new life?
2. How does prayer connect sorrow and joy in this passage?
3. Why does Jesus correct the disciples' overconfidence?
4. What makes Christian peace different from worldly calm?
5. How does the resurrection redefine our understanding of victory?
6. Where do you see Jesus' words "I have overcome the world" fulfilled today?

6

THE PRAYER OF GLORY
JOHN 17

Objective: To show how Jesus reveals God's glory through obedience, unity, and love-filled intercession.

INTRODUCTION

In 1741, composer George Frideric Handel locked himself in his study for 24 days. Servants brought him food he barely touched. When he finally emerged, he carried the manuscript of "The Messiah." Tears still on his cheeks, he said quietly, "I did think I did see all heaven before me, and the great God himself." Out of exhaustion came glory; from struggle came song.

John 17 captures an even greater moment—Jesus on the eve of suffering, yet speaking with the calm certainty of victory. The hour had come, but fear was absent. Instead, the Son lifted his eyes toward heaven and prayed. This was not the plea of a victim but the praise of a victor.

In this prayer, Jesus gathered every thread of the Gospel—glory, truth, love, and mission—and wove them into a single tapestry. He prayed for himself, for his disciples, and for all who will believe through them.

If Gethsemane reveals the agony of the cross, John 17 reveals its meaning. Here we see the Son glorifying the Father through obedience, the Father glorifying the Son through love, and believers drawn into that eternal glory. This is not just Jesus' prayer before dying—it's his declaration before reigning.

EXAMINATION

The Son glorified (17:1-5)

When Jesus lifts his eyes toward heaven and begins to pray, we are invited to overhear the holiest conversation in Scripture. The upper room had grown quiet. The farewell words were complete. Now the Son spoke to the Father—not as a teacher to his students but as a Son returning home.

"Father, the hour has come; glorify your Son that the Son may glorify you" (v. 1) The "hour," long anticipated throughout John's Gospel, had finally arrived. This is not an hour of disaster but of design—the moment when divine love will be displayed in full. In John's vocabulary, "glory" and "cross" are not opposites but synonyms. The crucifixion was not an interruption of glory; it was its unveiling.

The word "glory" (*doxa*) here signifies the visible radiance of God's nature. For Jesus to be glorified is for the Father's character—his love, mercy, and truth—to shine through the Son's obedience unto death. The Son did not seek applause but revelation: "Glorify me that I may glorify you." The mutual exchange of glory revealed the unity of their purpose.

Verse 2 expands the thought: "Since you have given him authority over all flesh, to give eternal life to all whom you have given him." Glory is expressed through giving. The Son glorified the Father by granting life to those the Father has entrusted to him. Eternal life is not merely endless existence but restored relationship—"that they know you, the only true God, and Jesus Christ whom you have sent" (v. 3)

This definition of eternal life transforms theology into intimacy. To "know" God is not to master information but to experience communion. Salvation, then, is not only escape from death's finality but also entrance into God's fellowship.

In verse 4, Jesus declared, "I glorified you on earth, having accomplished the work that you gave me to do." This was not presumption but completion. Before the cross was endured, its success was assured. The work given—revealing the Father, redeeming humanity—was as good as finished because obedience had carried it to the threshold.

Finally, Jesus prayed, "And now, Father, glorify me in your own presence with the glory that I had with you before the world existed" (v. 5). This is one of Scripture's most profound statements about the preexistence of Christ. The Son who took on flesh now asked to return to the glory he shared with the Father before time began. What the incarnation veiled, the cross would unveil.

This section opens the prayer with breathtaking perspective: eternity past, redemption present, and eternity future converged at the cross. The Son's path to glory ran through suffering; his crown was forged in the fires of obedience. The same pattern would mark every disciple who followed him.

The disciples kept and sanctified (17:6–19)

Jesus turned his attention from his own glorification to the preservation and mission of his disciples. "I have manifested your name to the people whom you gave me out of the world" (v. 6) To reveal the Father's name means to unveil his character. Through his words, miracles, and mercy, Jesus had made the invisible God visible.

The disciples, though slow to understand, had received and believed: "They have kept your word… they have believed that you sent me" (vv. 6–8). Their faith may have been fragile, but it was real. Jesus presented them to the Father as evidence that his earthly ministry had borne fruit.

Then comes the heart of the intercession: "I am praying for them. I am not praying for the world but for those whom you have given me" (v. 9). The distinction is not exclusionary but missional. Jesus prayed not that the world be ignored but that his followers would be equipped to serve it. To save the world, he had to first secure the witnesses who would proclaim salvation to it.

Verse 11 deepens the urgency: "I am no longer in the world, but they are in the world, and I am coming to you. Holy Father, keep them in your name, which you have given me, that they may be one, even as we are one." Jesus prayed for protection, not escape. The disciples were not to be withdrawn from the world but preserved within it. The phrase "keep them in your name" means to guard them by your character, to preserve their loyalty to your truth and love.

Their unity was not institutional but relational—"even as we are one." This oneness flowed from shared life in God, not from uniformity of opinion or structure. The unity Jesus envisioned is organic, like the unity of Father and Son: distinct persons, shared purpose.

In verse 12, Jesus looked back: "While I was with them, I kept them in your name... not one of them has been lost except the son of destruction." The reference to Judas underscores both divine sovereignty and human responsibility. Betrayal did not surprise Jesus; it fulfilled Scripture. Yet even in that loss, the Father's purpose moved forward.

Next, Jesus prayed for joy: "These things I speak in the world, that they may have my joy fulfilled in themselves" (v. 13). Joy, not fear, should characterize the Christian life. Even amid persecution, we are to experience the same joy that sustained Jesus—the joy of pleasing the Father.

But joy and conflict coexist. "I have given them your word, and the world has hated them because they are not of the world" (v. 14). The disciples' allegiance to truth inevitably invited hostility. Therefore, Jesus asked, "I do not ask that you take them out of the world, but that you keep them from the evil one" (v. 15). Protection replaced isolation. The church's holiness must exist in the tension of proximity and purity—engaged with the world yet distinct from it.

Verse 17 provides one of the prayer's most pivotal lines: "Sanctify them in the truth; your word is truth." Sanctification means to set apart for divine use. As the priests of old were consecrated with oil, Jesus' disciples are consecrated by truth. The Word shapes our identity and commission. Truth is not merely factual accuracy but God's revealed reality—the standard by which all else is measured.

Jesus grounded this sanctification in his own self-offering: "And for their sake I consecrate myself, that they also may be sanctified in truth" (v. 19). His impending death was not only substitutionary but also exemplary. As he was set apart for the cross, the disciples were set apart for service. The world would be reached through sanctified witnesses—those whose lives displayed the character of the One who sent them.

In these verses, the Great High Priest interceded for his priests-in-training. He prayed not that they be shielded from struggle but strengthened through it. Their holiness would be their greatest weapon, their unity their clearest witness, and their joy their most persuasive argument.

The church united and glorified (17:20–26)

Having prayed for the disciples before him, Jesus extended his vision across centuries: "I do not ask for these only, but also for those who will believe in me through their word" (v. 20). That includes every Christian since Pentecost—you, me, and all who have heard the gospel. This was Jesus' final intercession before the cross: a prayer for his church.

His first request is unmistakable: "That they may all be one, just as you, Father, are in me, and I in you, that they also may be in us" (v. 21). The purpose of this unity is evangelistic—"so that the world may believe that you have sent me." The credibility of the gospel rests not merely on its logic but on the love of its people.

This unity is neither institutional uniformity nor doctrinal minimalism; it is spiritual participation in the life of God. Jesus' earlier teaching about the vine and branches finds its fulfillment here. The same mutual indwelling that defines the Trinity now defines the church. When believers live in communion with Christ, they naturally live in communion with one another.

Verse 22 intensifies the thought: "The glory that you have given me I have given to them, that they may be one even as we are one." The glory shared between Father and Son is now entrusted to believers—not the glory of power but the glory of presence. God's indwelling Spirit becomes the bond of unity and the radiance of witness.

In verse 23, Jesus repeated the theme with new emphasis: "I in them and you in me, that they may become perfectly one, so that the world may know that you sent me and loved them even as you loved me." The world's conversion depends on the church's demonstration of divine love. The gospel must be proclaimed with words and proven in relationships.

Jesus then expressed his deepest longing: "Father, I desire that they also, whom you have given me, may be with me where I am, to see my glory that you have given me because you loved me before the foundation of the world" (v. 24). This is the ultimate purpose of redemption—not merely forgiveness, but fellowship; not just rescue from death, but reunion with glory.

Here Jesus lifted the curtain on eternity. The love shared between Father and Son before creation became the inheritance of the redeemed. Heaven is defined not by location but by communion—the people of God beholding the glory of God forever.

Verses 25–26 close the prayer with intimacy and continuity: "O righteous Father, even though the world does not know you, I know you, and these know that you have sent me. I made known to them your name, and I will continue to make it known, that the love with which you have loved me may be in them, and I in them."

The final words return to the opening theme: revelation and love. Jesus' mission was to make the Father known; his ongoing ministry, through the Spirit, continues that revelation. The end goal is love incarnate—divine affection dwelling within human hearts.

The phrase "I will continue to make it known" (v. 26) assures us that Jesus' prayer is still active. The Son's intercession did not end in Gethsemane; it continues in glory (Rom. 8:34; Heb. 7:25). Every Christian's perseverance is an answer to this prayer.

Theological reflection

John 17 is often called "The High Priestly Prayer" or "The Holy of Holies of the New Testament." Here, the curtain between heaven and earth momentarily parts, revealing the heartbeat of the Trinity. The Son prayed not for deliverance from death but for the Father's glory to be displayed through it.

Three currents flow through this chapter: glory, sanctification, and unity. Glory is the revelation of divine love through obedience; sanctification is the setting apart of believers by truth; unity is the visible outcome of both. The church's mission flows from this triune communion. Notice how the movement of prayer mirrors salvation history:

- From eternity to time (vv. 1–5): the Son descends to reveal the Father.
- From time to mission (vv. 6–19): the disciples are consecrated to carry the message.
- From mission to eternity (vv. 20–26): the church is gathered into everlasting fellowship.

This prayer ends where the Gospel began: "And the Word became flesh and dwelt among us, and we have seen his glory" (1:14). The glory revealed in Bethlehem's manger and on Calvary's cross would soon be revealed in the Father's presence and in the church's witness.

In the shadow of Gethsemane, Jesus was already interceding for his people. His final request before the cross was not for ease but for endurance, not for escape but for communion. The cross would answer the prayer for glory; Pentecost would answer the prayer for unity.

This "Prayer of Glory" reminds us that every act of obedience, every word of truth, every expression of love participates in this same divine mission. Jesus prayed not only for the first disciples but for all who would follow—and that includes us. We live today sustained by the echo of this intercession. The Son prayed for our perseverance before we ever learned to pray for it ourselves.

APPLICATION

1. Glory looks like obedience

Jesus prayed to be glorified through the cross—a request that redefined greatness forever. In a world obsessed with fame and success, he found glory in surrender. For believers, glory isn't recognition from others but reflection of the Father's character. Every act of obedience, however hidden, becomes radiant in heaven's eyes. When we forgive, serve, or remain faithful under pressure, we share in the Son's kind of glory. Obedience is not the cost of glory; it's the channel of it. The path to divine beauty still runs through humble faithfulness. If glory was revealed in Jesus' wounds, it will be revealed in our perseverance.

2. Unity begins with holiness

Jesus prayed that his followers would be one—but only after praying they'd be sanctified. True unity grows from truth, not apart from it. The church does not achieve unity by ignoring conviction but by aligning with God's character. When holiness shapes our hearts, love binds our lives. Division usually begins where sanctification is neglected. The Spirit unites only what truth has purified. A holy church will always be a united one because both flow from the same source: the Word that sanctifies. If we want the world to believe our message, we must embody the holiness of the One who sent us.

3. The mission depends on our love

Jesus' final prayer for future believers centers on love that proves the gospel's reality. The world will not be persuaded by our arguments but by our affection. Love is the apologetic the world can't refute. When the church mirrors the mutual care of Father and Son, it becomes living evidence of the message it proclaims. Every act of reconciliation, every bridge built across difference, preaches louder than a sermon. Evangelism without love is noise; unity without affection is hollow. The credibility of our witness rises and falls on how we treat one another. Christ's love in us is still God's chosen strategy for reaching the world.

4. We live between glory given and glory awaited

Jesus prayed that believers would see his glory—and, astonishingly, share it. That promise grounds our hope and shapes our daily perspective. Even now, his glory lives in us through the Spirit; one day, we'll behold it fully in his presence. The tension between "already" and "not yet" defines Christian life: we reflect glory now and await its perfection then. Every trial, sacrifice, and moment of faith moves us closer to that unveiled joy. The glory of eternity begins in the obedience of today. Until we see him face-to-face, our task is simple—to live as proof that his prayer is still being answered.

CONCLUSION

John 17 is the calm before the storm—the Son standing between eternity and the cross. His final request was not for escape but for glory, not for comfort but for communion. Every phrase reveals the heartbeat of heaven: that God would be known, his people would be holy, and his love would dwell among them. This prayer still echoes through the church today, sustaining every Christian who bears his name.

Yet the serenity of this moment soon gives way to chaos. Lesson 7 opens in the garden, where the prayer of glory meets the night of betrayal—and love kneels before hatred's hour.

REFLECTION

1. What does it mean for Jesus to be glorified through the cross?
2. How does knowing God define eternal life for you personally?
3. In what ways do you experience Jesus' prayer still being answered today?
4. How does sanctification prepare Christians for unity and mission?
5. What does "the glory given to believers" mean in your daily walk?
6. How can love reveal God's presence in a divided world?

DISCUSSION

1. Why does Jesus pray for glory before the suffering of the cross?
2. What's the difference between worldly success and divine glory?
3. How can holiness and unity coexist without compromise?
4. How does our unity influence the world's belief in Christ?
5. What practical steps help Christians reflect Christ's glory together?
6. How should the promise of future glory shape the church's mission today?

7

BETRAYAL & ARREST

JOHN 18:1-27

Objective: To show Jesus' sovereign obedience amid betrayal and reveal grace that restores fearful disciples.

INTRODUCTION

In AD 155, Roman authorities arrested an aging church leader named Polycarp. When asked to curse Christ and live, he replied, "Eighty and six years I have served him, and he has done me no wrong. How then can I blaspheme my King who saved me?" With calm dignity, he walked to his execution. The courage that steadied Polycarp was born in a garden long before—the night Jesus chose obedience over survival.

John 18 opens quietly but moves swiftly from prayer to betrayal. The peaceful rhythm of Jesus' words in chapter 17 gives way to the harsh clang of swords and shackles. Yet through every step, John insists on one truth: Jesus is in control. He speaks first, commands the soldiers, protects his disciples, and fulfills the Father's will. The scene looks like defeat, but heaven sees design.

This passage unfolds in three movements: Jesus' arrest, his questioning before Annas, and Peter's denial. Each reveals a different contrast—divine courage versus human fear, truth versus manipulation, faithfulness versus failure. The light of John 1 now flickers against the shadows of John 18, yet it never goes out. Even as Jesus is bound, his freedom shines brightest.

EXAMINATION

The garden of obedience (18:1–3)

After Jesus finished praying in John 17, he led his disciples across the Kidron Valley to a familiar garden. John's details are deliberate. The Kidron stream was stained by the blood of temple sacrifices flowing from the altar above. The one called "Lamb of God" now crossed those waters, stepping toward his own offering.

The garden setting links Eden with Gethsemane. In Eden, Adam fled from God and squandered his destiny; in this garden, the Second Adam embraced his to do the Father's will. What began with disobedience will end in obedience.

Judas arrived with a detachment of soldiers and temple police—a striking alliance of Rome and religion. John alone uses the word *speira*, suggesting a Roman cohort of several hundred men. The world's powers united against heaven's King (see Psa. 2:2). Judas, who once walked in friendship's circle, now approached under the banner of force. Yet no crowd or commander dictated what follows. The one they came to arrest is the one who governed their every move.

The sovereign "I Am" (18:4–11)

John makes clear that Jesus was no victim. "Then Jesus, knowing all that would happen to him, came forward and said to them, 'Whom do you seek?'" (v. 4). He did not hide or hesitate; he confronted the moment head-on. The same voice that once spoke the heavens and the earth into existence now addressed his captors.

Their reply—"Jesus of Nazareth"—invited a revelation. Jesus answered, "I am he." The Greek phrase *egō eimi* carries divine weight, echoing God's self-disclosure in Exodus 3:14: "I AM WHO I AM." John has used it repeatedly throughout his Gospel to identify Jesus as the self-existent Word made flesh.

At this declaration, the soldiers "drew back and fell to the ground." Power met divine presence, and human strength collapsed. No sword was drawn, no miracle performed—only words spoken, and the world's might bowed involuntarily. This was not chaos but choreography: even their posture fulfilled prophecy, testifying that no one took Jesus' life from him. He laid it down of his own accord (10:18).

Still, Jesus repeated the question to ensure his disciples' release: "If you seek me, let these men go" (v. 8). Even in arrest, he shepherded his flock. John notes that this fulfilled Jesus' earlier promise: "Of those whom you gave me I have lost not one" (v. 9). His concern remained protective, his authority intact.

Peter, unable to contain his loyalty, drew a sword and struck the high priest's servant, cutting off his right ear. The servant's name—Malchus—is preserved, perhaps because he later joined the Christian community that remembered this story. Jesus rebuked Peter: "Put your sword into its sheath; shall I not drink the cup that the Father has given me?" (v. 11).

The "cup" refers to the cup of divine wrath and the bitter necessity of the cross. Peter's violence revealed misplaced zeal. Courage without surrender quickly turns destructive. Jesus' true victory would come not through combat but through obedience. The garden of arrest became the theater of divine sovereignty: every step, every word, every wound unfolded by design.

The interrogation before Annas (18:12-14, 19-24)

The narrative shifts from open confrontation to quiet corruption. The soldiers and temple officers arrested Jesus and led him first to Annas, the father-in-law of Caiaphas, who was high priest that year. Though Caiaphas held the title, Annas held the power. Having served as high priest from AD 6-15, he still controlled the priestly hierarchy through his sons and sons-in-law. The shadow government of Jerusalem ran through his house.

John reminds readers that Caiaphas had earlier said, "It is better that one man should die for the people" (v. 14). What was meant as a political calculation now became divine fulfillment. The high priest spoke truer than he knew.

Inside Annas's residence, Jesus faced informal questioning—likely an attempt to gather evidence before the formal trial at dawn. "The high priest then questioned Jesus about his disciples and his teaching" (v. 19). But Jesus refused the role of defendant. "I have spoken openly to the world. I have always taught in synagogues and in the temple… Ask those who have heard me what I said to them" (vv. 20-21).

By appealing to witnesses, Jesus exposed the illegality of the interrogation. Jewish law required public evidence, not secret cross-examination.

His answer, calm yet courageous, placed his accusers on trial. When an officer struck him, Jesus responded, "If what I said is wrong, bear witness about the wrong; but if what I said is right, why do you strike me?" (v. 23). Dignity met violence. The One who could summon angels chose instead to stand firm in truth.

Annas, embarrassed and unprepared, sent him bound to Caiaphas. The true Judge stood accused, the true High Priest condemned by false priests. Yet in this darkness, the light of integrity still shone. Jesus' composure under injustice revealed the character of God himself.

Peter's denials (18:15–18, 25–27)

While Jesus stood firm inside, Peter crumbled outside. John interweaves their stories deliberately, contrasting steadfast truth with faltering faith. The unnamed "other disciple," known to the high priest, helped Peter gain entrance to the courtyard. As the servant girl at the gate challenged him—"You also are not one of this man's disciples, are you?"—Peter answered, "I am not" (v. 17).

The irony is painful. Only moments earlier, Jesus declared "I am," and men fell to the ground. Now Peter declared "I am not," and stood before a servant girl. Fear turns confession into denial.

Inside, Jesus bore witness; outside, Peter evaded it. While Jesus was struck for telling the truth, Peter lied to avoid the same fate. The contrast is deliberate: courage under pressure versus collapse under scrutiny.

Peter warmed himself by a charcoal fire—*anthrakia*—a detail John will later repeat in chapter 21, where Jesus restored Peter by another charcoal fire. For now, that warmth became an indictment against the apostle. Twice more Peter was asked if he was a disciple. Each denial deepened the fracture: first to a group of servants, then to a relative of Malchus who recognized his Galilean accent and his face. "Did I not see you in the garden with him?" (v. 26). Peter swore again, "I am not."

Immediately, a rooster crowed. The night split open with the sound of failure. But John's narrative leaves room for redemption. The crowing rooster did not signal the end of Peter's story; it marked the beginning of grace's pursuit.

APPLICATION

1. The garden calls us to obedience

The story begins where humanity once fell—in a garden. Adam hid; Jesus stepped forward. Every believer must decide which garden will define them: the one of rebellion or the one of surrender. Obedience may not remove suffering, but it redeems it. When Jesus crossed the Kidron, he chose God's will over his own comfort. The same invitation confronts us daily. Each act of submission, however small, echoes that holy night. The path of faith is rarely easy, but it always leads to life. When we choose obedience over escape, we stand beside Jesus in the garden, where the will of God still triumphs over fear.

2. Jesus is sovereign, even when bound

The soldiers fell backward at two words—"I am." Power belongs not to those holding weapons but to the one holding truth. John's picture of Jesus under arrest is a portrait of sovereignty disguised as surrender. When life feels out of control, it never is. The same Christ who orchestrated his own arrest still governs every circumstance today. Faith does not mean denying chaos; it means trusting the One who commands it. The cross wasn't forced upon Jesus—it was embraced. Our peace comes from remembering that nothing surprises a Savior who already stepped forward to meet the world's worst night.

3. Truth still stands on trial

The interrogation before Annas was less about evidence and more about silencing truth. Jesus refused to hide or compromise, insisting that his words had always been public. The world still prefers half-truths that make peace with darkness, but Christ calls his followers to speak with clarity and grace. Truth may be mocked, misunderstood, or struck—but it remains undefeated. When believers echo Jesus' integrity under pressure, they continue his testimony before the world. The courage to tell the truth—even when it costs—is one of the most important duties of the church. In a culture addicted to deception, honest faith still shines like light in a midnight courtyard.

4. Grace waits by every fire

Peter's denials show the gap between zeal and endurance, between loud promises and quiet fear. Yet failure is not final when grace is near. The rooster's crow marked Peter's collapse, but it also signaled that dawn was coming. Jesus' later restoration of Peter will prove that grace can rebuild what guilt has ruined. Many disciples still warm their hands by fires of compromise, afraid to be known. The good news is that Christ still seeks them. He does not shame the fallen; he restores them. The next time you feel like Peter—caught between loyalty and fear—remember: the same fire that revealed his failure later rekindled his calling.

CONCLUSION

John 18 opens the road to the cross with stunning contrasts—loyalty and betrayal, courage and fear, truth and deception. Yet through it all, Jesus remained unshaken. The same voice that calmed storms now steadied the chaos of his arrest. The Shepherd protected his sheep even as the wolves closed in. And Peter's failure, painful as it was, became proof that grace never quits.

The story now shifts from courtyard to courtroom. In Lesson 8, we stand before Pilate, where the world's power and heaven's purpose collide. There, the question will echo through history: "What is truth?"—and only one beaten, bound King will have the answer.

REFLECTION

1. What does Jesus' calm in the garden reveal about true obedience?
2. How does the "I Am" declaration shape your confidence in Christ's sovereignty?
3. Why is truth often resisted by those in power?
4. What lessons does Peter's failure teach about fear and faith?
5. How has Jesus' grace restored you after personal failure?
6. What does this passage teach you about courage under pressure?

DISCUSSION

1. Why does John emphasize Jesus' control during his arrest?
2. What makes the garden a fitting setting for redemption's beginning?
3. How can believers resist the temptation to fight with "swords" today?
4. What stands out in Jesus' response to Annas' questioning?
5. How does Peter's story give hope to failing disciples?
6. How can the church embody both truth and grace when under scrutiny?

8

BEHOLD THE MAN

JOHN 18:28-19:16

Objective: To show that Jesus' kingdom of truth exposes worldly power and demands our allegiance.

INTRODUCTION

In 1633, Galileo stood before the Roman Inquisition. Accused of heresy for claiming the earth revolved around the sun, he was ordered to recant or die. When he finally whispered, "And yet it moves," he affirmed a truth that outlasted his judges. History has a way of vindicating truth, even when power suppresses it.

John 18:28-19:16 tells of a far greater trial—one where Truth itself stood before the powers of the world. Pilate sat on Rome's marble bench; Jesus stood in chains. The Jewish leaders cried for blood while protecting their own ritual purity. The irony is staggering: those obsessed with defilement were the ones condemning the only sinless man.

Pilate's court became the stage where kingdoms collided—the empire of Caesar versus the kingdom of Christ, the politics of fear versus the reign of truth. Jesus would not argue or defend; he would define. His silence exposed corruption, his calm unmasked chaos, and his cross would soon reveal which king truly reigns.

This passage is not just history—it's a mirror. Every reader must decide, as Pilate did, what to do with the King who claims truth as his crown.

EXAMINATION

Jesus before Pilate (18:28–32)

The night had given way to dawn. After the chaos of the garden and the corruption of the high priest's court, Jesus was led to the Roman governor's palace. John notes that the Jewish leaders stopped at the threshold—they would not enter Pilate's Gentile headquarters "so that they would not be defiled, but could eat the Passover" (v. 28). That's some pretty thick irony. They were scrupulous about ritual purity while conspiring to kill the spotless Lamb. The hands that would not touch Gentile stone were already stained with innocent blood.

Pilate, annoyed by this early-morning intrusion, came out to meet them. "What accusation do you bring against this man?" (v. 29). The leaders dodged the question: "If this man were not doing evil, we would not have delivered him over to you" (v. 30). In other words, "Trust us—we've already decided his guilt." The exchange exposes the moral theater of the moment. Justice was a façade; the verdict was predetermined.

Pilate responded with irritation: "Take him yourselves and judge him by your own law" (v. 31). But they couldn't—Roman law forbade the Jews from carrying out executions. John notes that this fulfilled Jesus' own prophecy about the manner of his death: "to show by what kind of death he was going to die" (v. 32). Stoning was the Jewish method; crucifixion was Roman. Even the empire's machinery of death bent to divine design.

The stage was now set for a collision between two kingdoms—the politics of Rome and the purposes of heaven. Pilate stood as the representative of worldly authority; Jesus, the embodiment of divine truth. The trial that followed would reveal who was truly in charge.

My kingdom is not of this world (18:33–38)

Pilate retreated inside to question the prisoner himself. "Are you the King of the Jews?" (v. 33). The title drips with irony. The supposed king stood bound, bloodied, and abandoned. Yet his answer would redefine kingship forever.

Jesus replied with a question of his own: "Do you say this of your own accord, or did others say it to you about me?" (v. 34). He probed Pilate's heart. Was this inquiry political or personal? Was Pilate seeking truth or simply performing duty? The governor bristled: "Am I a Jew? Your own nation and the chief priests have delivered you over to me. What have you done?" (v. 35).

Jesus answered with words that have outlived empires: "My kingdom is not of this world. If my kingdom were of this world, my servants would have been fighting, that I might not be delivered over to the Jews. But my kingdom is not from the world" (v. 36).

His statement does not mean his kingdom has no presence on earth—it means it has no origin in it. His authority does not rise from armies or elections but from the Father's will. The words "of" and "from" mark the difference between divine sovereignty and human ambition. Earthly kingdoms advance by force; Christ's kingdom advances by truth.

Pilate, intrigued yet confused, pressed further: "So you are a king?" Jesus affirmed, "You say that I am a king. For this purpose I was born and for this purpose I have come into the world—to bear witness to the truth. Everyone who is of the truth listens to my voice" (v. 37).

Here stands the paradox of power: the prisoner before the throne is the true ruler; the judge on the dais was the one on trial. Jesus' kingship is grounded in revelation, not coercion. His subjects are those who trust and obey. His weapon is truth.

Pilate's reply is famous and tragic: "What is truth?" (v. 38). The words are not philosophical curiosity but weary cynicism. After years in politics, Pilate had seen too much spin, too many agendas. Truth to him was a tool, not a treasure. He spoke it and walked away, unwilling to wait for an answer. Yet Truth incarnate stood before him. The moment passed, and eternity grieved.

Behold the man (19:1–5)

Unable to find guilt but unwilling to lose favor with the crowd, Pilate attempted compromise. He ordered Jesus flogged. Roman scourging was brutal—leather thongs embedded with metal and bone tore flesh to ribbons. Many prisoners died before crucifixion even began. Soldiers, amused by the "King of the Jews," twisted a crown of thorns, pressed it onto his head, and draped him in a purple robe. Then they mocked him with the parody of the imperial salute: "Hail, King of the Jews!" (v. 3).

John's irony is deliberate. Every insult unintentionally affirmed truth. The thorns recalled the curse of Genesis; the robe anticipated the garments of glory; the sarcastic hail became worship in disguise. Even in mockery, creation bore witness: the King reigned from humiliation.

Pilate, perhaps hoping pity would suffice, brought Jesus out and declared, "Behold, I am bringing him out to you that you may know that I find no guilt in him" (v. 4). When Jesus stepped forward—bleeding, robed, crowned—Pilate said, "Behold the man!" (v. 5).

Those three words, meant as derision, have become proclamation: "Behold the man"—the true image of humanity, bearing our sin and shame. Here stood the Second Adam, clothed not in innocence lost but in suffering love. Pilate presented a broken man; God presented the world's Redeemer.

But pity does not soften hardened hearts. The chief priests and officers cried out, "Crucify him, crucify him!" (v. 6). Pilate's strategy failed because sin cannot be appeased; it must be atoned for.

No king but Caesar (19:6–16)

Pilate's frustration grew. He repeated, "I find no guilt in him." Yet the crowd's accusation escalated: "He has made himself the Son of God" (v. 7). This new charge alarmed Pilate. Roman superstition left room for divine men and omens; the idea that this prisoner might possess supernatural favor unsettled him. He reentered the praetorium, asking Jesus, "Where are you from?" (v. 9). But Jesus gave no answer. Silence became his final defense—fulfilling Isaiah's prophecy: "Like a lamb that is led to the slaughter… so he opened not his mouth" (Isa. 53:7).

Frustrated, Pilate asserted his authority: "Do you not know that I have power to release you and power to crucify you?" Jesus answered calmly, "You would have no authority over me at all unless it had been given you from above" (v. 11). With that statement, the hierarchy of history was reversed. Pilate was not in control; providence was. Even injustice operated under God's sovereignty.

From that moment, Pilate sought to release him, but political pressure intensified. The religious leaders played their final card: "If you release this man, you are not Caesar's friend. Everyone who makes himself a king opposes Caesar" (v. 12). The trap was complete. Loyalty to truth now threatened loyalty to empire. Pilate's career, already fragile, couldn't survive another complaint to Rome.

He brought Jesus out to the judgment seat at a place called The Stone Pavement (*Gabbatha* in Aramaic). John notes the time—"It was about the sixth hour, the day of Preparation of the Passover" (v. 14). As priests prepared lambs for slaughter, Pilate presented the Lamb of God. "Behold your King!" he declared. The words carried divine irony once again.

The response was chilling: "Away with him, away with him, crucify him!" Pilate asked, "Shall I crucify your King?" The chief priests answered, "We have no king but Caesar" (v. 15). In that sentence, covenant history collapsed. The leaders who prided themselves on monotheism publicly pledged allegiance to Rome. The rejection of Christ was complete.

So Pilate, trapped between conscience and convenience, "delivered him over to them to be crucified" (v. 16). His name now forever tied to cowardice, he sealed the most unjust verdict in history. Yet even this injustice served the justice of God. What men meant for political expedience, heaven used for redemptive victory.

What became of Pontius Pilate?

After the events of the Gospels, Pilate continued to govern Judea for several more years. Ancient historians such as Josephus and Philo record that his rule grew increasingly tense; he provoked Jewish unrest by using temple funds for Roman projects and by suppressing protests with violence. Around AD 36–37, after a bloody incident in Samaria, Pilate was recalled to Rome to answer for his actions before Emperor Tiberius. Tradition diverges after that point. Some early writers say he was dismissed and exiled; later Christian sources claim he took his own life. Whatever the details, Pilate's story ends much as it began—troubled, compromised, and far from peace. Scripture leaves him frozen in that moment of indecision, asking, "What is truth?" His tragedy reminds every generation that neutrality toward Jesus is itself a verdict.

APPLICATION

1. Truth is not an idea but a Person

Pilate's question—"What is truth?"—still echoes across every age. The world treats truth as opinion, but Jesus defines it as himself. To know truth is to know him. Followers of Christ don't merely argue facts; they follow a King whose words reveal reality. Pilate's tragedy was standing face-to-face with truth and walking away unchanged. We repeat his mistake whenever we seek comfort more than conviction. True faith does not ask, "What is truth?" but "Who is Lord?" When we listen to Jesus' voice, confusion finds clarity and chaos meets peace. The world's cynicism cannot outshout the calm authority of a Savior who still says, "Everyone who is of the truth listens to my voice."

2. Compromise is the enemy of conviction

Pilate knew Jesus was innocent, yet fear of Rome silenced his conscience. One accusation—"You are no friend of Caesar"—undid his integrity. Moral collapse rarely happens overnight; it begins with small concessions to comfort and the crowd. Pilate reminds us that neutrality before truth is impossible. To avoid a decision about Jesus is to make one. Christians cannot serve both Christ and convenience. Every generation faces its own pressure to bow before lesser kings—career, popularity, politics, or peacekeeping. But loyalty to truth always costs something. Will we protect our position or follow our King? Pilate washed his hands; the disciple must take up Christ's cross.

3. The King reigns from the place of shame

When Pilate presented Jesus with the words, "Behold the man," he spoke more than he knew. The bleeding figure before him was humanity's truest image—majestic in mercy, glorious in suffering. The crown of thorns crowned our redemption. The purple robe mocked him but proclaimed his divine royalty. Christ's kingship overturns every worldly definition of strength. His victory comes through vulnerability. When believers endure suffering with faith, they join in that same paradoxical reign. The world may see weakness, but heaven sees worship. To follow a crucified King is to believe that redemption often wears a crown of thorns.

4. Allegiance has only one throne

The chief priests cried, "We have no king but Caesar!" Their words reveal humanity's deepest temptation—to trade the eternal for the immediate. Whenever comfort, security, or approval outranks obedience, we repeat that cry. The cross exposes our divided loyalties and calls us back to singular devotion. Christ does not share thrones; he claims them. The gospel demands a decision: Caesar or Christ, compromise or confession, convenience or conviction. The irony is that those who bowed to Caesar were destroyed by the very empire they served, while those who bowed to Christ gained a kingdom that will never fall. Allegiance to Jesus may cost us everything—but it secures us forever.

CONCLUSION

The trial before Pilate revealed the world at its worst and God at his best. Power trembled before truth, politics bent before purpose, and the Judge of all creation stood accused so that sinners might be acquitted. Pilate washed his hands; Jesus stretched out his. The one who seemed powerless would soon sit at the right hand of the Majesty in heaven.

But the story, of course, is not over. Lesson 9 moves from the courtroom to the hill of execution. There, the crown of thorns becomes the crown of glory, and the King who was condemned will make his final declaration: "It is finished."

REFLECTION

1. Why do you think Pilate asked, "What is truth?"
2. How does Jesus' silence reveal both strength and submission?
3. What does it mean that Christ's kingdom is "not of this world"?
4. How can you avoid Pilate's mistake of compromise?
5. Where have you seen truth mocked but still victorious?
6. What rivals compete with Jesus for your ultimate allegiance?

DISCUSSION

1. How does Pilate embody the conflict between conscience and convenience?
2. Why is truth essential to understanding Jesus' kingship?
3. What modern examples echo the crowd's cry, "We have no king but Caesar"?
4. How can believers display Christ's kingship in a skeptical culture?
5. What does "Behold the man" teach us about God's view of strength?
6. How does this passage challenge our ideas about power and glory?

9

THE CRUCIFIXION OF THE KING

JOHN 19:17-42

Objective: To show how Jesus' death fulfills Scripture, completes redemption, and reveals God's sovereign love.

INTRODUCTION

In 1968, Swiss artist Georges Rouault painted a crucifixion unlike any other. Christ is centered, but the background is not a hill or a sky—it's a throne room. Gold and crimson light surrounds the cross. Rouault explained, "The cross is not defeat. It is the coronation of love."

That is the message of John 19. The Roman governor, the priests, and the soldiers all thought they were mocking a powerless man. But John invites us to look deeper: this is the moment when the true King was lifted up, not in shame, but in glory. The throne was a cross; the crown was of thorns; the coronation words were, "It is finished."

Every detail carries meaning. Pilate's inscription preached truth he didn't understand. The soldiers' dice fulfilled a prophecy they don't know. And the garden tomb—so still, so near—awaited a dawn it couldn't imagine.

John wants us to see that Jesus' death is not the end of his mission but the completion of it. The cross is not where God lost control—it's where he displayed it most. The crucifixion is the victory no one saw coming: the King reigning through love that would rather die than let sinners go.

EXAMINATION

The King lifted up (19:17–22)

The long night of betrayal, trials, and denials had ended. Now morning dawned with a different kind of coronation. John's Gospel never uses the word "Golgotha" to evoke horror—it uses it to reveal glory. "So they took Jesus, and he went out, bearing his own cross, to the place called the Place of a Skull" (v. 17). The condemned man carried the instrument of his death, as kings once carried their scepters. What Rome intended as humiliation, heaven ordained as hope.

John notes that Jesus "went out." The phrase recalls Old Testament sacrifices taken outside the camp, bearing reproach for the people (Lev. 16:27; Heb. 13:12). The Lamb left the city so that sinners might enter it clean. Even his path fulfilled prophecy.

Pilate, still stung by his earlier defeat with the priests, nailed a title above the cross: "Jesus of Nazareth, the King of the Jews" (v. 19). It appeared in Hebrew, Latin, and Greek—the languages of religion, empire, and culture. The inscription that was meant to mock instead proclaimed the universal gospel: this King rules over every tribe and tongue.

The priests protested, demanding Pilate revise the title to read, "This man said, I am King of the Jews." But Pilate, weary and bitter, replied, "What I have written I have written" (v. 22). His stubbornness became prophecy. The banner above the cross declared an eternal truth: the rejected Nazarene is the world's rightful King. Rome thought it has crushed a rebel; God was enthroning a Redeemer.

The soldiers and the seamless garment (19:23–24)

Beneath the cross, soldiers carried out the mundane business of execution. Four men divided Jesus' garments among themselves, fulfilling the custom that allowed an execution squad to claim a prisoner's clothes. But one piece remained—a tunic woven in one piece from top to bottom. "Let us not tear it, but cast lots for it to see whose it shall be" (v. 24).

John pauses to note that even this fulfilled Scripture: "They divided my garments among them, and for my clothing they cast lots" (Psa. 22:18). Nothing about this moment was accidental. The Scriptures Jesus came to fulfill were unfolding stitch by stitch.

The seamless tunic may also carry symbolic meaning. Jewish readers would remember the seamless garment worn by the high priest (Exod. 28:31–32). John's Jesus is both sacrifice and priest—the one who offered and the one offered. Even in death, his unity remained intact. The garment remained unbroken, just as his body would soon be—against expectation—left unbroken on the cross.

The soldiers gambled for clothing; heaven prepared a robe of righteousness. The King reigns, not in silks and jewels, but in blood and love.

Behold your son, behold your mother (19:25–27)

As the soldiers gambled, a small cluster of faithful hearts remained near the cross. John lists four women: Mary the mother of Jesus, her sister (likely Salome), Mary the wife of Clopas, and Mary Magdalene. Among them stood the beloved disciple. Amid agony, Jesus' gaze found them.

"When Jesus saw his mother and the disciple whom he loved standing nearby, he said to his mother, 'Woman, behold, your son!' Then he said to the disciple, 'Behold, your mother!'" (vv. 26–27).

In this moment, Jesus did what Adam failed to do—he protected and provided. Even while bearing the world's sin, he remembered personal love. He entrusted his mother not to extended family but to a disciple defined by affection. The cross not only reconciled humanity to God; it also created a new family among believers.

From that hour, John writes, "The disciple took her to his own home." The church began at the foot of the cross—not in power but in compassion. Jesus' final acts of love on earth were relational, not regal.

"I thirst" and "It is finished" (19:28–30)

John is meticulous about fulfillment. "After this, Jesus, knowing that all was now finished, said (to fulfill the Scripture), 'I thirst.'" (v. 28). The One who turned water into wine, who offered living water to the Samaritan woman, now experienced dry mouth. He thirsted not only from physical exhaustion but also from bearing sin's desolation. Psalm 69:21 foresaw this moment: "They gave me sour wine to drink."

A jar of sour wine sat nearby, the cheap vinegar drink of soldiers. They lifted a sponge to his lips on a branch of hyssop—the same plant used to sprinkle Passover blood on Israel's doorposts (Exod. 12:22). Every symbol aligned: the Lamb of God, lifted up, the blood applied, judgment passing over.

When Jesus received the wine, he declared, "It is finished" (v. 30). The Greek word *tetelestai* was a cry of triumph, not defeat. In commerce, it meant "paid in full"; in the context of mission, "accomplished." The same root appears in 17:4—"I have finished the work you gave me to do." The cross was not failure; it was fulfillment. Every prophecy, every promise, every shadow of the old covenant found completion here.

John adds one last detail: "He bowed his head and gave up his spirit" (v. 30). No one took his life; he yielded it. The crucifixion was not the moment God lost control—it was the moment love took command.

The pierced side (19:31–37)

The Jews, anxious to remove the bodies before the Sabbath, asked Pilate to have the legs of the crucified men broken—a brutal act that hastened suffocation. The soldiers complied with the two thieves but, finding Jesus already dead, they pierced his side instead. Immediately, "blood and water came out" (v. 34).

John, ever the eyewitness, insists on this detail: "He who saw it has borne witness—his testimony is true" (v. 35). The flow of blood and water has inspired centuries of reflection. Physically, it confirmed real death; spiritually, it signified cleansing and life. Blood symbolizes atonement; water symbolizes the Spirit. The same elements that flowed from his body would soon flow into his church—sacrificial forgiveness and spiritual renewal.

Two Scriptures find fulfillment here: "Not one of his bones will be broken" (Exod. 12:46; Psa. 34:20) and "They will look on him whom they have pierced" (Zech. 12:10). The first affirmed him as the flawless Passover Lamb; the second anticipated Israel's repentance and the world's worship.

Even in death, Jesus governed every detail. No bone was broken, no prophecy overlooked, no word unfulfilled. The spear that sought to confirm his death instead confirmed his identity.

The burial of the King (19:38–42)

When the spectacle ended and the crowd dispersed, two quiet figures stepped into the scene—men who once followed from the shadows. "After these things Joseph of Arimathea, who was a disciple of Jesus, but secretly for fear of the Jews, asked Pilate that he might take away the body of Jesus" (v. 38).

Pilate consented, and Joseph, joined by Nicodemus, brought a mixture of myrrh and aloes—about seventy-five pounds. The extravagance of the amount signaled devotion worthy of a king. Nicodemus, who first visited Jesus under cover of night (3:1–2), now stepped into daylight. Grace had emboldened timidity.

They wrapped the body in linen with spices, "as is the burial custom of the Jews" (v. 40). John notes the location: "Now in the place where he was crucified there was a garden, and in the garden a new tomb" (v. 41). The setting was no accident. Humanity's story began in a garden where death was born; it would be reborn in a garden where death would die.

The tomb was new—unused, uncontaminated—fit for the body of the sinless one. They laid him there because the Sabbath was near. The narrative closes with stillness: no thunder, no miracle—just rest. The Lamb who cried, "It is finished," now rested from his work. Creation waited for the third day's dawn.

APPLICATION

1. The cross is our throne of grace

John shows us not defeat, but enthronement. The King reigns from a cross, turning a symbol of shame into glory. Every Christian who kneels before that throne finds mercy, not judgment. Pilate's inscription—"King of the Jews"—was meant to mock, yet it proclaims what faith confesses: Jesus is King. The cross reminds us that God rules through self-giving love. Our victories come the same way—not by control, but by surrender. When we bear our own crosses, we share in his reign. Every act of humility, every sacrifice for love's sake, becomes a royal moment. The path to glory still runs through obedience.

2. God's word is always fulfilled

John's passion narrative beats with one refrain—"that the Scripture might be fulfilled." Even as soldiers gamble, prophecy is kept. Even as enemies mock, God's plan unfolds. The cross is proof that no promise of God will ever fail. What looks chaotic to men is coordinated by heaven. When life feels uncertain, we remember Calvary: every word spoken by God will stand. The fulfillment of Scripture in Jesus' death guarantees the faithfulness of Scripture in our lives. We can trust his timing because we've seen his track record. The Bible isn't just true—it's trustworthy. If God kept his word at the cross, he will keep it in our valleys too.

3. Love creates a new family

At the cross, Jesus united those who loved him most and least. He looked at his mother and his disciple and said, "Behold your son… behold your mother." In that moment, he founded a community shaped by compassion, not bloodlines. The cross doesn't just reconcile sinners to God—it reconciles them to each other. Every Christian household, friendship, and church becomes a living echo of that moment. We care for one another because we have been cared for by him. The family of God was born beneath a blood-stained tree, where grace bound strangers together. To follow Christ is to love as he loved, to serve as he served, and to stand beside one another at the foot of his cross.

4. The work is finished, but faith must respond

When Jesus cried, "It is finished," he closed the account of sin forever. Nothing can be added; nothing remains unpaid. Yet faith must still receive what grace has completed. Many try to earn what's already been given, chasing peace that was bought long ago. The gospel calls us to rest, not perform. Our obedience is gratitude, not payment. "It is finished" means our past cannot condemn us and our future cannot fail us. The only unfinished work now is ours—to believe, to bear witness, to live like people who are free. The King has done his part; the question is whether we'll live in the victory he declared.

CONCLUSION

John 19 brings heaven's plan to its climax. The King who carried his own cross now reigned from it, declaring that redemption's work was complete. Every prophecy found fulfillment, every symbol found substance, every sinner found hope. The cross was not the end of Jesus' mission—it was the center of God's story.

But love's triumph was not yet fully seen. The King had been buried, the tomb was sealed, and the world grew still. In Lesson 10, we will step into the dawn of a new creation—where grief gives way to glory, and the One who said "It is finished" will rise to say, "Peace be with you."

REFLECTION

1. How does the cross redefine what glory looks like?
2. What does "It is finished" mean for your faith today?
3. Where do you see God fulfilling his promises in your life?
4. How does the cross shape your relationships with other believers?
5. What emotions surface when you picture Jesus saying, "I thirst"?
6. How can the cross steady you in seasons of uncertainty?

DISCUSSION

1. What does John emphasize about Jesus' control during his crucifixion?
2. Why is the title "King of the Jews" theologically significant?
3. How does John's fulfillment theme strengthen faith in God's sovereignty?
4. What do the blood and water symbolize for Christians today?
5. How do Joseph and Nicodemus model courage for modern disciples?
6. Why does John close the crucifixion story with a garden and a tomb?

10

RESURRECTION

JOHN 20:1-18

Objective: To show that resurrection faith begins with personal encounter and leads to joyful witness.

INTRODUCTION

Early in the 20th century, a painter named Eugene Burnand captured one of Scripture's most intimate moments—the race of Peter and John to the tomb. In the painting, both men are running, eyes wide, wind pressing against their faces. But if you look closely, you'll notice what fills their expressions most: hope mixed with fear. They are running toward something they cannot explain but cannot ignore.

That's exactly where John 20 begins—on the edge of dawn, with love outrunning certainty. Mary Magdalene, still heavy with grief, went to the tomb expecting to find death. Instead, she found absence. The stone was rolled away, but understanding hadn't yet dawned.

John's resurrection account isn't about fireworks; it's about encounter. There were no earthquakes or trumpets—only a voice speaking a name. The same Jesus who called Lazarus from the tomb now called Mary from despair.

In this passage, we move from darkness to light, from confusion to confession. And at the center stands one word that changes everything—"Mary." The risen Christ turned mourning into joy and transformed the seeker into the first messenger of Easter.

EXAMINATION

The empty tomb (20:1–10)

The Gospel that began with light shining into darkness now opens its final act "while it was still dark" (v. 1). John's description is both literal and symbolic: darkness still clung to the world's understanding even as the light of resurrection began to rise.

Mary Magdalene came early to the tomb—not expecting a miracle, but to mourn a memory. She had stood near the cross and watched him die; love for her Lord brought her back to the place where hope was buried. But when she arrived, the stone had been rolled away. No angels sang. No trumpets sounded. Just absence.

Her immediate reaction was not faith but fear: "They have taken the Lord out of the tomb, and we do not know where they have laid him" (v. 2). Resurrection was not yet on her radar. Like all disciples, she interpreted what she saw through the lens of loss.

Peter and the "other disciple," traditionally understood as John, ran to the tomb. The younger disciple outran Peter and stooped to look in. He saw linen cloths lying there but did not enter. Peter, typically impulsive, rushed in and observed the same scene—burial clothes neatly arranged, the face cloth folded and set apart. This detail suggests not theft but order. No grave robber folds laundry.

Then John entered, saw, and believed (v. 8). What exactly did he believe? Likely that Jesus had risen, though he still didn't understand how. John notes, "For as yet they did not understand the Scripture, that he must rise from the dead" (v. 9). Faith preceded full understanding. He believed before he comprehended, trusting the evidence of grace more than the explanation of logic.

The two disciples then returned home, leaving Mary alone by the tomb. The empty space had not yet spoken hope to her heart. Her story—and ours—reminds us that the resurrection is not discovered by speed but by staying. Some run and reason; others weep and wait. Jesus would meet both.

Weeping and wonder (20:11–13)

"But Mary stood weeping outside the tomb" (v. 11). Her perseverance in grief became the doorway to revelation. Tears often blur our vision but can sharpen our faith. When sorrow holds us still, grace can finally find us.

As she wept, Mary stooped to look into the tomb. She saw two angels in white, sitting where the body of Jesus had lain—one at the head and one at the feet. The arrangement evoked the mercy seat atop the ark of the covenant, flanked by cherubim (Exod. 25:18–19). The place of sacrifice had become a place of mercy.

The angels asked her, "Woman, why are you weeping?" (v. 13). The question was tender but probing. Heaven's messengers were not seeking information—they were inviting interpretation. Why weep where victory has begun? Mary replied with raw honesty: "They have taken away my Lord, and I do not know where they have laid him." Her words echo humanity's deepest lament—loss of presence. She called him "my Lord," even when she believed him gone. Faith clings to the One it loves before it understands the life he gives.

The gardener and the name (20:14–16)

Turning around, Mary saw someone standing behind her. "She did not know that it was Jesus" (v. 14). Resurrection was not recognized by sight alone; it required revelation. The last time she saw him, his face had been bruised and bloodied. Now, transformed by glory, he stood alive, yet hidden by her tears.

Jesus asked the same question as the angels, adding another: "Woman, why are you weeping? Whom are you seeking?" (v. 15). The repetition is deliberate—grief must be confronted before joy can be received. Mary assumed he was the gardener. The irony is divine: she is correct without knowing it. In Genesis, Adam was placed in a garden to tend creation; now the Second Adam stood in a garden to renew it. Resurrection is new creation breaking through old soil.

"Sir, if you have carried him away, tell me where you have laid him, and I will take him away." Her love spoke of impossibility—one woman carrying a man's corpse—but love rarely calculates feasibility.

Then came the turning point: "Jesus said to her, 'Mary'" (v. 16). One word. One name. And the darkness ended. The voice that called creation into being now called her back to faith. As in John 10, the Shepherd called his sheep by name, and they recognized his voice.

She turned fully toward him and exclaimed in Aramaic, "Rabboni!"—meaning "my Teacher." The possessive form reveals intimacy. Jesus was not just *the* Teacher; he was *hers*. Recognition comes from relationship. Resurrection faith begins when we realize we are known.

Do not cling to me (20:17)

Mary's instinct was to embrace him. Love wants to hold what it almost lost. But Jesus said, "Do not cling to me, for I have not yet ascended to the Father." His words were not a rebuke of affection but a redirection of faith.

Jesus was not forbidding touch—he would invite Thomas to do so later (20:27). Rather, he was teaching that the relationship had changed. Before the cross, his presence was local and physical; after the resurrection, it would be spiritual and universal. Mary had to release the old form of fellowship to receive the new.

His next command revealed the purpose of resurrection: "Go to my brothers and say to them, 'I am ascending to my Father and your Father, to my God and your God.'" (v. 17). This is the first time Jesus called the disciples "my brothers." The cross had closed the gap between Master and servant, Creator and creature. His Father has become their Father. The Son's resurrection inaugurated the Christian's adoption.

Notice also the tense: "I am ascending." The resurrection was not an endpoint but a passage. The risen Lord pointed forward to exaltation. His mission was not complete until he brought humanity back into the Father's presence. Mary, who came seeking a body, became the first messenger of glory.

"I have seen the Lord" (20:18)

Mary obeyed. The first witness of the resurrection was not Peter or John, not a scholar or priest, but a woman whose testimony would not have been legally admissible in court in her culture. Heaven overturned human hierarchy again. The one once called "possessed by seven demons" became the first to proclaim resurrection. Grace chooses the unlikely so that glory belongs to God.

She went and announced to the disciples, "I have seen the Lord." Her statement was both personal and theological. She didn't say, "The tomb was empty," or "The angels spoke." She spoke of encounter, not evidence.

Her declaration fulfilled Jesus' promise in 16:22: "You will have sorrow now, but your hearts will rejoice, and no one will take your joy from you." Her weeping had turned to witness. Her darkness had turned to dawn.

In John's Gospel, sight often symbolizes faith (1:14; 9:25; 14:9). Mary's vision—seeing and believing—is the foundation of the church's commission. Her voice carried the first Easter sermon: "I have seen the Lord." It's not a conclusion reached; it's a relationship regained.

APPLICATION

1. Resurrection faith begins with relationship

Mary's tears turned to joy when she heard her name. The first sound of Easter wasn't thunder or trumpet—it was a voice saying, "Mary." Faith is always personal before it becomes public. We don't meet an idea at the empty tomb; we meet a person who knows us. Resurrection faith doesn't demand proof—it responds to presence. The Savior who called her still calls us by name, awakening trust in hearts dulled by grief. You may not understand everything about resurrection life, but you can recognize the voice of the One who brings it. Faith doesn't begin with clarity; it begins with encounter. The risen Lord still whispers names in the darkness, and that is enough to make morning break.

2. Grief can be the doorway to grace

Mary stayed when others left. She wept when others wondered. And because she stayed, she saw. Sometimes faith requires not strength but stillness—the courage to remain when all hope seems buried. The angels' question, "Why are you weeping?" wasn't a rebuke but an invitation to look deeper. Our tears often reveal what we love most. Jesus meets us in those tears, not after them. Resurrection doesn't deny grief; it redeems it. The same sorrow that blinded Mary became the place where grace appeared. In seasons of loss, staying near the tomb in prayer—staying near the place of confusion—often leads to unexpected revelation. God still turns weeping into wonder.

3. Let go of what was to receive what is

When Mary recognized Jesus, she instinctively clung to him, but he said, "Do not hold on to me." Resurrection changes how we relate to him. He is no longer confined by time or place; he is now always present. Many believers still reach for yesterday's version of Jesus—old comforts, old experiences—when he is calling us into something new. Faith must release the past to embrace the fullness of the risen Christ. Spiritual maturity means learning to hold loosely what was so we can receive what is. The Christ who once walked beside us now lives within us. The One who once stood in the garden now reigns in glory. We can't cling to the way he was when he's calling us to see who he is.

4. Resurrection turns witnesses into messengers

Jesus' first command after resurrection was not to build a monument but to share a message: "Go to my brothers and say to them…" Mary's encounter became her commission. The truest evidence of resurrection isn't an empty tomb—it's a changed life that speaks. Every believer who has "seen the Lord" becomes a messenger of hope. Like Mary, we move from weeping to witnessing, from holding to heralding. The gospel spreads through voices once silenced by sorrow. Jesus entrusts his victory not to the powerful but to the faithful. He calls us to go where fear still reigns and speak peace into darkness. Resurrection faith is not meant to be admired—it's meant to be announced.

CONCLUSION

John's resurrection story began in darkness but ends in dawn. Mary came seeking a body and found a risen Savior who called her by name. Her sorrow became a sermon, her tears became testimony, and her silence turned into proclamation: "I have seen the Lord." The same voice that met her in the garden still speaks into our grief and confusion, calling each of us to faith and duty.

But the story of resurrection doesn't end at the tomb. In Lesson 11, Jesus will meet his frightened disciples behind locked doors, turning their fear into peace and their doubt into purpose. The risen Lord still sends his people out with joy.

REFLECTION

1. What does Mary's persistence teach you about seeking Jesus in grief?
2. What does Jesus' use of Mary's name reveal about the nature of his love?
3. What emotions does the phrase "It was still dark" stir in you?
4. How does Jesus transform your understanding of loss or disappointment?
5. What does "Do not cling to me" mean for your walk with Christ?
6. Where might Jesus be sending you to share your "I have seen the Lord"?

DISCUSSION

1. Why does John highlight Mary as the first witness to the resurrection?
2. How does the "gardener" image connect resurrection to new creation?
3. Why do faith and understanding often grow at different speeds?
4. What does Mary's encounter reveal about the personal nature of faith?
5. How does this story reshape our response to sorrow and waiting?
6. What does it look like to move from weeping to witnessing today?

11

PEACE BE WITH YOU

JOHN 20:19-31

Objective: To show how the risen Christ replaces fear with peace and doubt with faith.

INTRODUCTION

During World War I, on a quiet Christmas Eve, soldiers in opposing trenches laid down their weapons. Across No Man's Land, a single voice began singing "Silent Night." One by one, others joined until enemies were singing together. For a few fleeting hours, peace broke through the smoke of war.

That moment, as fragile as it was, gives us a glimpse of what Jesus offered in John 20. The disciples were not on a battlefield, but their hearts were at war—with fear, guilt, and confusion. The doors were locked, the future uncertain, and faith was fading fast. Then Jesus came and stood among them and said, "Peace be with you."

This was no temporary truce but lasting reconciliation. The One who bore their sins now breathed new life into their souls. His wounds became their proof, his breath their power, his words their commission. And to one doubter, he offered not shame but sight, turning skepticism into the strongest confession in John's Gospel: "My Lord and my God."

In this lesson, we move from fear to faith, from locked doors to open hearts. The risen Christ still enters our chaos, still speaks peace, and still sends his followers into the world made new.

EXAMINATION

Peace in a locked room (20:19-23)

Fear is a terrible architect. The disciples had built their refuge with locks and silence. It was evening on the first day of the week—the same day Mary saw the risen Lord—and yet they hid behind bolted doors "for fear of the Jews" (v. 19). They had heard the good news, but terror has a louder volume than faith.

Then, without announcement or sound, "Jesus came and stood among them." No key turned, no door opened. The One who passed through death now passed through walls. His first word was not rebuke but reassurance: "Peace be with you." This greeting fulfilled his promise from 14:27—"My peace I give to you." It was more than calm emotion; it was covenant restoration. The peace of Christ is not the absence of danger but the presence of the risen Lord.

He showed them his hands and his side. The marks of suffering were not erased but glorified. His scars were his credentials—proof that the crucified one and the risen one are the same person. The resurrection did not undo the cross; it vindicated it. When they saw, they rejoiced (v. 20). Fear yielded to worship.

Again he said, "Peace be with you." Repetition turned greeting into commissioning. "As the Father has sent me, even so I am sending you" (v. 21). The risen Christ did not gather his followers merely to comfort them but to send them. Mission, not maintenance, defines resurrection community. The pattern is unmistakable: the Father sent the Son; the Son now sent the church. The same divine movement of love that began in heaven now continues on earth.

Verse 22 completes the picture: "And when he had said this, he breathed on them and said to them, 'Receive the Holy Spirit.'" The verb recalls Genesis 2:7, when God breathed life into Adam. Now the Second Adam breathed new creation into his disciples. What sin once drained of life, the Spirit now restored. The resurrection was not just resuscitation; it was re-creation.

Then comes a puzzling statement: "If you forgive the sins of any, they are forgiven them; if you withhold forgiveness from any, it is withheld" (v. 23). This is not priestly power to absolve but apostolic authority to announce. The disciples' mission (and ours) was to proclaim forgiveness through the name of Jesus. Where the gospel is received, sins are released; where it is rejected, sins remain. The church does not create forgiveness—it carries it. Jesus equips his people to extend the peace they have received.

In this brief encounter, Jesus transformed fear into faith and disciples into missionaries. The room once filled with dread became the birthplace of the church.

The absent disciple (20:24–25)

Thomas was not there. We are not told why. Maybe grief drove him to isolation; maybe disillusionment sent him walking. Either way, he missed the meeting that changed everything. When the others told him, "We have seen the Lord," he could not echo their joy. Their testimony sounded like fantasy to ears tuned to realism.

Thomas's skepticism has earned him the nickname "Doubting Thomas," but doubt in Scripture is rarely pure unbelief—it is wounded faith. His words were honest, not cynical: "Unless I see in his hands the mark of the nails, and place my finger into the mark of the nails, and place my hand into his side, I will never believe" (v. 25).

He wanted certainty, not conspiracy or speculation. His demand mirrored Jesus' earlier display to the others (v. 20). Thomas asked only for the same assurance they already received. His doubt was not rebellion; it was longing. Faith that never wrestles rarely deepens.

The patient Savior (20:26–29)

Eight days later, the disciples were again indoors. The doors were still locked—old habits die hard—but Jesus came and stood among them just as before. The first words were the same: "Peace be with you." The risen Christ met fear with consistency. His peace does not fade with time.

Then he turned directly to Thomas. There was no reprimand, only invitation: "Put your finger here, and see my hands; and put out your hand, and place it in my side. Do not disbelieve, but believe" (v. 27). Jesus met him at the exact point of his doubt. Grace was specific. He repeated Thomas's own words back to him as if to say, "I heard every syllable." The same patience that sought Peter in failure now sought Thomas in uncertainty.

The text never says Thomas touched him. Perhaps the sight of the wounds was enough. What began as a demand became a declaration: "My Lord and my God!" (v. 28). This is the Gospel's highest confession of faith. John began his narrative with, "The Word was God," and now it concludes with a disciple proclaiming the same. What the prologue asserts, Thomas affirmed.

Jesus replied, "Have you believed because you have seen me? Blessed are those who have not seen and yet have believed" (v. 29). The beatitude reaches across centuries to every reader. Faith that trusts the testimony of Scripture is not second-class faith; it is the blessed norm of the new age. The kingdom would not be built on repeated appearances but on enduring belief.

Faith for the future (20:30–31)

John pauses here to tell us why he wrote: "Now Jesus did many other signs in the presence of the disciples, which are not written in this book; but these are written so that you may believe that Jesus is the Christ, the Son of God, and that by believing you may have life in his name."

This is both conclusion and invitation. The signs recorded—water to wine, blind eyes opened, a dead man raised—were not random miracles; they were revelations of identity. John was not collecting evidence for curiosity's sake but offering testimony for faith's sake.

Two verbs define the goal: "believe" and "have life." Belief in John's Gospel is never static; it is a continual posture of trust. Life is not mere survival but participation in divine fellowship. The Gospel began with "In him was life" (1:4); it ends with that life extended to all who believe.

Notice also the shift from eyewitnesses to readers. Thomas saw and believed; future believers would read and believe. The written word now mediates the living Word. The Spirit who breathed on the disciples now breathes through the pages of Scripture, producing the same peace and faith in every generation.

APPLICATION

1. Jesus enters our locked rooms

Fear still builds walls—around hearts, homes, and churches. The disciples locked their doors to stay safe, but Jesus came through anyway. His presence isn't stopped by fear; it walks straight into it. The same Lord who entered that room now enters our anxieties, doubts, and failures with the same words: "Peace be with you." His peace is not escapism; it's invasion—God breaking into human fear with divine calm. When Jesus stands among us, our security no longer depends on circumstances but on presence. Resurrection peace doesn't come by avoiding danger but by welcoming the Savior who already conquered it.

2. The Spirit breathes life into our mission

When Jesus breathed on the disciples, it wasn't symbolic—it was transformative. The same Spirit that gave life to Adam now empowers God's people for mission. Christianity is not sustained by adrenaline or strategy but by breath—the Spirit's continual renewal. Every believer lives between two breaths: God's creation breath that made us and Christ's resurrection breath that remakes us. Evangelism, forgiveness, and compassion all flow from this divine respiration. The Spirit is not a distant power but the nearness of God's life within us. Every time we exhale grace into the world, we echo that first moment when Jesus breathed peace into the fearful lungs of his followers.

3. Doubt can lead to deeper faith

Thomas wanted evidence, but what he received was an encounter. His doubt was not the enemy of faith; it became its doorway. Jesus did not shame him for questioning; he invited him to see, touch, and believe. Doubt dealt with in the presence of Christ becomes dialogue, not disaster. Many Christians hide their uncertainties, thinking them disqualifying. But the risen Christ specializes in meeting doubters with mercy. Honest questions can mature faith faster than shallow certainty ever could. The goal is not to erase doubt but to let grace answer it. The same hands that welcomed nails now welcome the hesitant. Our faith deepens when we bring our wounds to the One who still bears his.

4. Faith must become confession

Thomas's story ends with one of Scripture's greatest declarations: "My Lord and my God!" True faith cannot remain internal—it speaks. Belief becomes worship when it names Jesus rightly. The resurrection demands response instead of silence. Thomas's confession joins the chorus begun in John 1: "The Word was God." Every Christian must echo that cry personally: "My Lord"—the one I follow—and "My God"—the one I adore. Faith without confession is admiration; faith with confession is allegiance. To say "My Lord and my God" is to surrender ownership of your life and entrust it to the risen King. Jesus' final blessing—"Blessed are those who have not seen and yet believed"—belongs to all who make that same confession today.

CONCLUSION

The story of Thomas and the locked room reminds us that the risen Jesus still enters fearful places. His first word is always peace, his first act always grace. He meets us where we are—behind walls of worry, within rooms of doubt—and transforms them into sanctuaries of faith. His breath still fills the church; his wounds still proclaim victory.

But the gospel story isn't finished. In Lesson 12, the risen Lord will walk beside his followers again—this time by the sea. There, around another fire, grace will restore a fallen disciple and remind us that peace leads to purpose, and forgiveness always calls us forward.

REFLECTION

1. What fears has Jesus entered and transformed in your life?
2. How does Jesus' peace differ from the world's version of peace?
3. What does it mean for you to be "sent" as Jesus was sent?
4. How has the Spirit breathed new life into your faith recently?
5. When have your doubts led to deeper faith instead of distance?
6. What personal confession echoes Thomas's words, "My Lord and my God"?

DISCUSSION

1. Why are Jesus' first words to his disciples "Peace be with you"?
2. How does the resurrection shape the church's mission in the world?
3. What does the "breath of the Spirit" teach about new creation?
4. Why is Thomas's doubt essential rather than embarrassing for faith?
5. How does Jesus' blessing in verse 29 extend to today's Christians?
6. What does this passage teach us about the relationship between faith and sight?

12

DO YOU LOVE ME?
JOHN 21

Objective: To show how Jesus restores failure through love and renews disciples for faithful service.

INTRODUCTION

After Thomas Edison's laboratory burned to the ground in 1914, destroying years of research, the inventor's son found him watching the blaze. Edison calmly said, "Go get your mother and all her friends—they'll never see a fire like this again." Then, with resolve, he added, "It's gone. But tomorrow we'll start rebuilding."

That spirit of restoration runs through John 21. The Gospel doesn't end with triumph in Jerusalem but with breakfast on a beach. Peter, who once promised loyalty and delivered denial, had returned to what was familiar—fishing. The risen Christ met him there, not to shame him but to rebuild him.

Around another charcoal fire, the smell of his failure still lingered. Yet this time, grace was cooking breakfast. Jesus asked three questions that cut deeper than guilt: "Do you love me?" Each answer became restoration and recommission.

John 21 reminds us that resurrection isn't just about empty tombs—it's about renewed hearts. Jesus doesn't merely forgive the fallen; he entrusts them with his work. Love for Christ must become care for others, and grace received must become grace given. On this final shoreline, the story of the Gospel came full circle: the first call—"Follow me"—was also the last.

EXAMINATION

Jesus by the sea (21:1-6)

The resurrection had already changed everything—and yet, for the disciples, life felt strangely the same. Days had passed since the locked-room appearance, but the future remained uncertain. Jesus had risen, yes, but what came next? In that confusion, Peter decided to do what he knew best: "I am going fishing" (v. 3). The others joined him, and together they spent a long, unfruitful night on the Sea of Galilee.

John's details are not wasted. The empty nets mirrored the disciples' emptiness of purpose. Resurrection truth had not yet become resurrection vocation. When dawn broke, a figure stood on the shore. "Children, do you have any fish?" (v. 5). The question sounds ordinary, but in John's Gospel, divine revelation always begins with everyday words. Their reply—"No"—was an admission of failure that opened the door to grace.

Then came the command: "Cast the net on the right side of the boat, and you will find some" (v. 6). Obedience turned futility into abundance. The nets filled so rapidly that they could hardly haul them in. The scene recalls Luke 5, the first miraculous catch that called Peter to discipleship. The same miracle that began their journey now renewed it. The difference? Previously, Jesus called them to become fishers of men; now he restored them to that purpose after failure.

The miraculous catch and recognition (21:7-14)

"That disciple whom Jesus loved therefore said to Peter, 'It is the Lord!'" (v. 7). Peter nose-dived into the sea, swimming toward the shore. The water that once threatened to drown him now carried him toward redemption.

When the others arrived, dragging the net, they found Jesus standing beside a charcoal fire with fish and bread already prepared (v. 9). The detail is crucial. The last time Peter stood near a charcoal fire, he denied his Lord (18:18). Now he would be restored beside one. Jesus recreated the setting of Peter's failure, not to shame him but to heal him.

John notes that the net was "full of large fish, 153 of them" (v. 11). The number has sparked endless speculation, but John's point is simpler: the catch was both vast and intact. "Although there were so many, the net was not torn." The unbroken net symbolizes the unity of the church's commission. In Luke 5, the nets broke; in John 21, grace held them together. What began as a fishing story became an allegory for our gospel work—abundant, diverse, and held fast by divine strength.

When Jesus invited them, "Come and have breakfast," (v. 12) the moment became almost domestic. The risen Lord was not a distant figure of glory but a host who feds his friends. He took bread and gave it to them, echoing the feeding of the five thousand and the Last Supper. John notes, "None of the disciples dared ask him, 'Who are you?' They knew it was the Lord" (v. 12). Faith had matured beyond curiosity. Resurrection presence no longer needed explanation—it inspired recognition and worship.

The scene is gentle, unhurried, and ordinary—and that is precisely its wonder. Resurrection doesn't just happen in temples or tombs; it happens at breakfast, on beaches, in the quiet return of love to those who feel unworthy of it.

Peter's restoration (21:15–19)

After breakfast, Jesus turned to Peter. The conversation was both intimate and public; Peter's denial had been public, and so his restoration had to be too.

"Simon, son of John, do you love me more than these?" (v. 15). The question cut through bravado and comparison. Once Peter had declared, "Even if all fall away, I never will" (Mark 14:29). Now Jesus asked, "Do you love me more than these?"—perhaps meaning more than the other disciples, or more than fishing, or more than his old life. The ambiguity fit Peter's divided heart.

Jesus asked Peter three times, using two verbs—*agapaō* and *phileō*—that in John's Gospel carry no sharp distinction. Both express genuine love and devotion. The conversation was not a test of vocabulary but of heart. Each exchange linked affection to action: "Feed my lambs… Tend my sheep… Feed my sheep." In Jesus' kingdom, love is not sentimental; it is sacrificial. The one who once boasted of loyalty was now called to quiet service.

When Jesus asked the third time, Peter was grieved—not because of a change in wording, but because he remembered his denial. "Lord, you know everything; you know that I love you" (v. 17). The disciple who once trusted his own strength now appealed to Jesus' knowledge. Grace had turned pride into dependence. Jesus said, "Feed my sheep." The shepherd imagery evokes Ezekiel 34, where God promised to raise a true shepherd for his people. Peter's ministry would now continue that mission.

But restoration came with realism. "Truly, truly, I say to you, when you were young, you used to dress yourself and walk wherever you wanted, but when you are old, you will stretch out your hands" (v. 18). John explains: "This he said to show by what kind of death he was to glorify God" (v. 19). The one who once feared suffering would one day embrace it. Love would take Peter where pride never could.

Finally, Jesus said again what he said years earlier beside another sea: "Follow me" (v. 19). Restoration is not a return to the past; it is a renewed beginning.

The question about the beloved disciple (21:20–23)

As Peter turned to follow, he noticed "the disciple whom Jesus loved" trailing behind—the same one who had leaned against Jesus at the Last Supper. Peter asked, "Lord, what about this man?" (v. 21). Old habits die slowly. Comparison crept back even in a moment of grace.

Jesus answered sharply but kindly: "If it is my will that he remain until I come, what is that to you? You follow me!" (v. 22). The repetition of "you" emphasized focus. Peter's call was personal, not comparative. The Christian life is never measured by another's path but by faithfulness to one's own.

A rumor later spread among the early church that this beloved disciple would not die before Jesus returned. John corrects it in verse 23: "Jesus did not say to him that he would not die, but, 'If it is my will that he remain until I come, what is that to you?'" The misunderstanding illustrates how easily truth can become rumor when speculation replaces obedience. The risen Lord called his followers not to decode the future but to walk faithfully in the present.

The testimony and purpose (21:24–25)

The Gospel closes not with a grand epilogue but with quiet assurance: "This is the disciple who is bearing witness about these things, and who has written these things, and we know that his testimony is true" (v. 24).

John's self-reference serves two purposes. First, it identifies the beloved disciple as the eyewitness behind the narrative. Second, it underscores the reliability of the Gospel's testimony. Faith is not built on rumor or legend but on firsthand encounter verified by community. "We know that his testimony is true." The plural "we" suggests the early church's confirmation of John's eyewitness testimony.

Then comes the closing flourish: "Now there are also many other things that Jesus did. Were every one of them to be written, I suppose that the world itself could not contain the books that would be written" (v. 25).

The hyperbole captures the boundless nature of Christ's work. John has not exhausted the story; he has opened it. The same risen Lord who fed disciples by the sea still feeds believers through his Word. The Gospel ends not with closure but with invitation—to keep following, to keep loving, to keep bearing witness to the Light that has overcome the darkness.

APPLICATION

1. Grace finds us where we fail

Peter returned to fishing not because he stopped believing, but because he stopped knowing what to do next. Failure often sends us backward. Yet Jesus met him in the same place where it all began—same sea, same nets, same call. Grace doesn't avoid our failures; it enters them. The risen Christ doesn't wait for perfect disciples—he restores broken ones. Every believer has a shoreline where shame still whispers, but Jesus stands there too, cooking breakfast and inviting conversation. The gospel's power is not that it erases our past but that it transforms it into testimony. Grace always finds us where we fell so it can send us forward again.

2. Love is proven in service

When Jesus asked Peter, "Do you love me?" he followed each affirmation with an assignment: "Feed my sheep." True love for Christ cannot remain sentimental; it must become practical. To love the Shepherd is to care for his flock. Every act of compassion, every word of encouragement, every burden borne for another is an answer to that same question. Christian ministry is not performance—it's affection expressed through service. The Lord still asks, not for eloquence or success, but for love that labors. Our success or effectiveness is measured not by the crowds we attract but by the people we feed. Love without service is noise; service without love is exhaustion. Only when both unite does the church reflect its risen Shepherd.

3. Comparison is the thief of calling

Peter's first question after restoration was, "Lord, what about this man?" Grace had restored his heart, but envy was already tugging at it. Jesus' answer—"What is that to you? You follow me"—remains one of the most liberating commands in Scripture. The greatest threat to obedience is distraction. Each Christian's path is unique; comparison only breeds insecurity or pride. We cannot follow Jesus while glancing sideways. Our focus must stay on the One ahead, not the one beside. The question of "What about them?" must always give way to "What about me, Lord?" Faithfulness is not measured by someone else's assignment but by our own obedience. The risen Christ calls each believer to walk the path of grace designed specifically for them.

4. Restoration always leads to mission

The chapter ends not with Peter's apology but with his commission. Jesus' forgiveness is never an endpoint—it's a launching point. He restores us not just to heal us but to send us. "Feed my sheep" was Peter's invitation to join the ongoing work of the kingdom, just as ours is today. Every forgiven heart becomes a vessel for grace. The church's story begins here—around a fire, in forgiveness, among the ordinary. When we experience restoration, we also receive responsibility: to share what we have seen, to serve where we have been saved. Resurrection life is not meant to be admired from the shore but lived in the deep. Forgiven people must become sent people, carrying the warmth of that same charcoal fire into a cold world.

CONCLUSION

John's Gospel ends where it began—with a simple invitation: "Follow me." The story that started by the sea concludes by the same shore, where grace rebuilt what failure had broken. Peter's denials were not the final word. The risen Jesus doesn't discard broken disciples—he restores them and trusts them again.

Every Christian stands with Peter, hearing that same question: "Do you love me?" Our answer is not proven in words but in how we feed, tend, and follow. The Gospel of John closes not with farewell, but with commission—the living Christ still calling his followers to love deeply, serve faithfully, and keep walking behind him until the story is finished in glory.

REFLECTION

1. When has Jesus met you in a place of failure or regret?
2. What does Jesus' question "Do you love me?" stir in your heart today?
3. How can you show love for Christ through service this week?
4. Where are you tempted to compare your journey with someone else's?
5. What does Peter's restoration teach you about grace and second chances?
6. How does this story invite you to follow Jesus more personally and faithfully?

DISCUSSION

1. Why did Jesus repeat his question to Peter three times?
2. What is significant about the charcoal fire in this passage?
3. How does Peter's restoration redefine leadership and ministry?
4. What lessons can we learn from Jesus' command "Feed my sheep"?
5. Why does comparison threaten our obedience to Christ's call?
6. How does John 21 connect resurrection faith with everyday mission?

www.ingramcontent.com/pod-product-compliance
Lightning Source LLC
Chambersburg PA
CBHW070155080526
44586CB00015B/1993